National Service

"Two Years of My Life"

✳

By JIM RITCHIE

Copyright © 2014 by Jim Ritchie

All rights reserved. No part of this publication may be reproduced, stored in a retrieval system, or transmitted, in any form or by any means, electronic, mechanical, photocopying, recording, or otherwise, without the written prior permission of the author.

ISBN: 978-1500552749

Typeset in Book Antiqua with Arial display at SpicaBookDesign

Printed with www.createspace.com

Table of Contents

1 My Call to Arms and A Sad Good Bye..........1

2 Fort George................................17

3 Troopship to Afar..........................38

4 Good luck in Hong Kong.....................50

5 Back with my Squadies......................71

6 Life on a Hilltop..........................82

7 Rest and Recuperation.....................111

8 Leaving the D.M.Z.........................130

9 Britannia Camp and Pusan..................137

10 Ho Tung House............................148

11 Troopship Devonshire and Home............164

12 Redford Barracks and Freedom.............174

Afterword....................................181

ONE

My Call to Arms and A Sad Good Bye

The picture on the cover of this book was taken several months before I was called up into the Army to begin my National Service. As I look at that picture after all these years, I see a happy and contented young man who had just finished his apprenticeship and was a fully fledged carpenter with a skill level so honed that he thought that he could make just about anything out of wood.

My self-imposed five years of night-school (two and three evenings a week) was over, and I was in possession of a valuable piece of paper, (valuable only to me) which stated that I had passed the "Final" City and Guilds of London Institute exam on Building Construction. With this certificate I believed mistakenly that doors would open in my quest to advance myself to a well paid job, which would result in having more spending money, of the folding type, in my pocket. I was hoping that with this newly found income, I would be able to concentrate on the two things that interested me most at that particular time in my life: Girls and Dancing. These two pursuits have been on the back burner for too long, for I was unable to indulge in such pleasurable pursuits simply because I had neither the time nor the money to engage in any romancing.

From the age of twelve, when I joined a youth organization called The Boy's Brigade, I had been involved in a pipe band. I was given a practice chanter along with a 'Logan's Tutor' and told that I was to be one of the pipers in a new band that was being formed. This band was brought into being by one of the young officers, John Stevenson, who played the pipes by ear and couldn't read a note of music. Six young boys were given 'Logan's Tutors' and were expected to teach themselves to read bagpipe music. In this we were assisted by an elderly gentleman in town; a piper, who would sit with us for an hour each week, helping to make sense of it all.

It was an uphill battle for the boys; they lost interest and dropped out one by one. My Mother came to the rescue and told me that if I really wanted to play the pipes, I would have to take private lessons, and she knew just the man who would help me. So with my parents help, I carried on with piping on my own, and by the time I was fifteen, I was able to play reasonably well. It was then that I was asked to take on the task of teaching five young boys in the Boys Brigade to play this ancient instrument, so that the pipe band could get restarted This was quite a commitment for me, trying to keep up the boys' interest and enthusiasm, so that after a few years we could eventually have a band that could go on parade with a repertoire of a dozen or more tunes. This teaching and the encouraging that these young boys needed to keep them going through the tough parts of learning, took a lot of my time, and for several years I devoted at least one evening a week to this.

As well at this time, my interest in woodwork knew no bounds, and I was forever making bits of furniture, model boats, etc. and I even made a wood turning lathe out of some lumber and old bicycle parts. This lathe was powered by hand; by someone hand cranking a bicycle pedal connected to a series of gears and chains and belts, every turn of the bicycle pedal resulting in the lathe turning fifty revolutions I was very proud of this piece of mechanical ingenuity that I had put together, and I managed to turn several table lamps and indian clubs on it before I ran out of manpower, or I should say boy-power, for the neighbourhood boys whom I called upon to turn the pedal-handle soon ran out of interest. I was left to dream of an electric motor that would do this work.

All through my teenage years I was captivated by the "Big Band" sounds, and of the saxophone in particular. I mentioned to my Dad that I was very keen on playing the saxophone but he didn't seem the least bit interested in what I was talking about, even though I said that I would pay for the lessons. He seemed even less interested when I told him that I didn't have enough money to purchase a very inexpensive sax that I could get for five pounds, and if I waited until I had saved up the money to buy it, the sax would be gone by then. After hearing this from me he was still silent and I thought that the matter was dead; so it surprised me when a few days later he said to me: "I tell you what Jim, if you pass the City and Guilds exam that is coming up, I will think about paying for half of that saxophone that you talked about... what did you say it was going to cost?" I said "It's an old used alto sax that the music teacher with whom I was hoping to take lessons from has for sale, and he is asking five pounds". My Dad said "It's a deal, but you have to pass the exam first." That was all the incentive I needed, and in a short time I had in my possession an old, well worn alto sax that had a reasonably good sound.

My music teacher, Joe Fry, was the leader of a small dance band. Joe lived in the outskirts of Glasgow, about thirty five minutes by bus from my home. My love affair with the saxophone had began, and with my musical experience of several years playing the pipes, my progress at playing this new instrument was rapid. Joe was very much impressed with me and asked if I would be interested in joining his dance band once I was more proficient with the instrument. This was indeed music to my ears and a whole

NATIONAL SERVICE: "TWO YEARS OF MY LIFE"

new dimension to my life came suddenly into focus. The only negative thought that came to my mind clouding this new dimension was that if I was playing these wonderful tunes in a dance band, how would I be able to dance with those lovely girls seen on the dance floor. It was a pleasant dilemma, but it didn't curb my enthusiasm for I knew that sooner or later a solution to that problem would be found.

Such was the state of my affairs when this picture was taken; I knew that National Service was just around the corner and I would be receiving notice from the authorities soon after my twentieth birthday. Several of my friends were already in the Forces doing their time, and I was actively corresponding with them. John Barrett was in Germany as part of the Occupation Forces, and from what he was writing me, he was having the time of his life and really enjoying himself while stationed at Wiesbaden, near the Austrian Alps. My other friend, Jim Ferguson, was in the Air Force stationed somewhere in England; he was not so enthusiastic about his lot and had fears of developing stomach ulcers from all the "lousy" food served. It was certainly disrupting to their lives, but neither seemed to be complaining too much, so perhaps when my turn came I could get a cushy posting to some exotic paradise…..I was always prone to dreaming in Technicolor.

✴

Two weeks before my 20th birthday, on the 6th of December 1950 I received notification to report to the local Ministry of Labour Office to register for National Service. This was my first notice, and I found out later that many men had escaped enlistment because they decided to disregard this notice, and were able to slip through the cracks to avoid National Service. They must have been braver than I, for accompanying the notice was a warning that anyone disregarding the call to register would be dealt with harshly by the authorities, and face imprisonment. After reading that, I meekly reported to the Ministry of Labour office and registered.

A week later another buff coloured envelope arrived at our house. It was a letter requesting me to report to a hospital in Glasgow for chest x-rays. This was not unexpected as the West of Scotland was in the midst of a TB epidemic, and many young people were dying of this incurable (1950) disease. I was recently exposed to it, as Andy, one of my young pipers had just recently been diagnosed with TB and was now confined to bed in a sanatorium. Andy and I had swapped chanters on many occasions during our piping practice sessions while neither of us were aware of his condition. This letter now ordering me to have an X-ray made me think that they would probably discover that I also had the disease; a chilling thought to contemplate. A week later another letter came, ordering me to report to the same hospital in Glasgow for another X-ray, so by now I was almost convinced that I had TB and could actually feel ghost like pains in my chest -- such was the power of negative thinking.

I attended the hospital again and had several X-rays taken. There was some small comfort in knowing that if I did indeed have TB, then I would be excused from National Service, but I fervently hoped that this would not be the case. I wanted to be healthy and would be more than happy to do my National Service.

A few days later I was again informed by letter to report to a hospital in Glasgow on December 26, Boxing Day,(which like Christmas Day was not then an official holiday in Scotland) where I would have a medical examination to assess my physical condition and suitability to become a member of His Majesty's Armed Forces.

The die was cast and the date set; I would soon know how fit I was, or otherwise ... I could again feel that dull, ghost like pain in my chest.

I decided to get my medical early in the morning of the 26th so that I could work in the afternoon and not lose a full day's pay at the construction site where I was working at the time.

My Dad would leave for work every morning at about 7:15; he would walk or catch a local bus to take him up a short distance to Main Street in Barrhead, where he would take another bus going south, arriving at the grocery store where he worked. I would catch another local bus that came fifteen minutes after the one my Dad had taken, and when it reached Main Street, I would then transfer to a bus going north to Glasgow.

The morning of the 26th was cold and frosty, and I was aboard the local bus as planned, on my way for my medical, when the bus unexpectedly made a quick stop to pick up someone who had flagged it down. Everyone looked up to see who was getting on the bus, and I recognized a young woman who worked in the store beside my Dad. She looked very distraught and when she spotted me, she ran up and said, "I knew that you would be on this bus Jim, your Dad told me; you have to get off at the next stop, your Dad has had a bad turn".

A chill ran through me and I thought that my Dad has never had a bad turn, what could have happened?

The bus stopped and I jumped off to see a crowd gathered around someone who was sitting propped up against the old building adjacent to the bus stop. Parting the crowd, I saw that it was my Dad, the hero of my life, his eyes closed and a trickle of blood formed at the corner of his mouth. I knelt down in front of him, held his head in my two hands and cried in anguish "Dad, speak to me!" while gently clapping his cheek. The crowd around me was silent. I felt for his pulse, and when I could feel none, I knew that my Dad's life was over. This single and most traumatic event in my life affected me greatly, for it made me love and revere my Dad in a way that I may not have been able to had he lived to a ripe old age. To this day, I think of my Dad as the greatest man I have ever known, and one, who by example, made me think and act as I do.

It seemed like a cruel coincidence that my Dad had died on the doorstep of the only undertaker in Barrhead; the establishment of 'Charlie Roberts Funeral Undertaker'. Charlie was a good friend of my Dad, and as I stood up I realized that he was standing right beside me. He was just as shocked as were the people standing there, some of whom I recognized as more of my Dad's friends.

Charlie said to me "It's all over for your Dad Jim, so let's carry him into my place and I will take care of everything." Several men came forward, and we carried my Dad in and laid him gently on a long table in Charlie's' place.

The events of the last few minutes had left me in shock, I couldn't speak. Charlie took me by the shoulders and said "Look at me Jim." I looked into his face and he said "Jim, I will look after all the arrangements here and I want you now to go home to tell your Mother and everyone else what has happened today". As it can be imagined, this was by far the most difficult and grievous task that I had ever been called upon to do. I was still in shock as I left Charlie's place and I decided to walk the mile home and try to come to terms with what had just happened.

Eventually I reached our house, consumed by grief but keeping it in check as much as possible. I opened the front door and stepped into the hall; my Mother came out of the kitchen and asked" Have you forgotten something Jim?" By the look on my face, she knew right away that something was wrong. I said, "I have bad news Mum." Her face turned white and I blurted out. "Daddy just had a fatal heart attack."

I remember my Mother's words clearly: "No, no, it's just a bad dream." We hugged for a long while, then she turned and went into her bedroom and closed the door; she was overwhelmed by grief.

Despite how wretched I was feeling, it was now up to me to get the word out, and I spent the next several hours giving the sad news to as many of our family members as I could contact by phone and then by walking, or taking the bus to their homes. My Aunt Jessie and Uncle Alex, who lived close by were the first to know. Aunt Jessie was my Mother's younger sister and Uncle Alex had been my Dad's closest friend since boyhood. Since they had married sisters, Alex Bell became my Uncle Alex and they were our closest family friends.

Uncle Alex told me not to worry about anything as he would check with Charlie Roberts and look after all the funeral arrangements; Aunt Jessie and he would come over in the afternoon to see and console my Mother. Uncle Alex was a wonderful uncle and close friend, and he did much to comfort and console me at this time. By early afternoon I was back home; my little sister Grace and my Grandfather were there and Mother was bravely trying to cope when she told me that I had better go to Glasgow and keep that appointment with the Services Medical Board, or I would be breaking the law and might be sent to prison. Such was the great respect we had for the law in those days.

Was it intimidation, naivety or whatever that made me go on that day of all days for an examination that could, and should have been postponed for another day? This was a pivotal day in my life but I didn't realize it at the time because I was ignorant of many of the rules and regulations of this Medical that I had been ordered to attend. I found out many years later that if I had phoned the Services Medical Board and told them that my Father had just died, I would have been excused National Service on the grounds that my Mother was now a widow. Not knowing this, I left home, caught a bus and travelled to Glasgow for that all-important medical exam to find out if I had TB, or not.

Arriving at Stobhill Hospital in Glasgow, I realized that I was not the only one to get examined that day, for I joined a line up of young men my age who were there for the same reason. The clerk who interviewed me had my folder close at hand, they were obviously expecting me; he checked all my personal information, then handed me the folder and said "Take this with you." then pointed to a large door and told me to go through there. This door led into a small hall with benches at one end that held small bundles of clothing. At the other end of the hall were three small tables at which three men in white, obviously doctors, were examining young men stripped down to their shorts, coming forward from the short line-up that had formed. I was told to do the same by leaving my clothes on the bench, picking up my folder and joining the line.

This scene looked vaguely familiar and I realized that in some of the war movies that I had recently seen, young men like us had been going through this same routine prior to joining the Army, and here I was part of that same scene.

I soon found myself before one of the doctors who gave me the standard medical exam: blood pressure, pulse, reflexes, soundings which included the lungs. I was expecting him to say something, but he was silent and continued with his examination, writing all his findings in my folder. No questions were asked and no words were spoken until he said "OK., that is it, you can get dressed now and then go through the door at the end of the hall where you will wait in the ante-room there until your name is called. When that happens, you will be interviewed by the Chief Medical Officer who will inform you the results of this medical ... Next !"

I waited on a bench in this ante-room for some time; one man would come out of the door marked Chief Medical Officer, the door would close and soon after a name would be called, prompting a young man to stand up and go in for his report. To pass the time I engaged in conversation with the two young men in front of me on the bench. All of us were concerned what our examination would reveal about our general physical condition, and joked what this might find. Eventually the name of the young man, who was two ahead of me was called, and in he went. A short time later he came out and we jokingly asked him: "Well, did they find anything." "Yes, they did…..from my X-ray they found that I have T.B. and I am now being sent to a sanatorium." Then he added with a wry smile. "There will be no National Service for me."

This revelation was a shocker for me and the fellow sitting beside me; it was no joking matter, people ware dying of TB and this great fear that I had of having the dreaded TB myself, could soon be revealed. If my deadly fear was confirmed, coupled with what already happened this morning, I was afraid to think of how I would react emotionally, for at this time my Father's death was weighing heavily on me.

The young lad in front of me in the line had his name called, he stood up and I wished him good luck. In he went and I waited with bated breath to hear what the result of his examination might have revealed When he came out, I asked: "How did it go in there?" He said with a half smile. "I had a mastoid in my ear last year which left me deaf in that ear so I have now been exempt from National Service." I think he was glad and relieved at that decision; he smiled at me and said "Good luck in there," pointing to the door that he had just came from and which was now closed.

I was next, and when "James Ritchie" was called, I held my breath and walked in. The Chief Medical Officer was sitting behind his desk with my folder in front of him, an empty chair in front of his desk. He said "Hello James, please have a seat."

I sat down and he continued. "I have just read your medical report James, and I am happy to tell you that you are a fine and healthy specimen of a young man, the kind that I am weaning out of all of those who came before me today. As you are no doubt aware, our country's Armed Forces have many commitments around the world, and the forces, mainly our Army, needs constant replenishment of people. At the present time the 1st Battalion of the Argyll and Southern Highlanders is in Korea, attached to the United Nations Forces who are trying to prevent South Korea from falling into Communist hands."

I knew instinctively what was coming next as he said "I am going to recommend you to be assigned to that famous and distinguished regiment to complete your two years' of National Service. Do you have any comment to make, James?"

Taken by surprise, I blurted out what had been occupying my mind for several weeks now. "Sir, with regard to my chest X-ray, I was asked to go in for a second time, and I was under the impression that I had some sort of a lung infection, possibly TB"

He quickly looked at my documents in front of him and said "There is nothing to worry about James, the first X-Ray was blurred and they only needed a backup. Now if that is all James, then I will finish off our interview by telling you that you will be receiving notice in the mail in a few weeks time as to where you will report for duty to commence your National Service. Good luck James."

I didn't know whether to laugh or cry; all I knew for sure was that there would be no 'cushy' two years' posting for me.

Looking back at that moment in my life, I have often thought that all I had to say to this Chief Medical Officer was that my Father had died that morning, and my Mother was now a widow. For just saying that, I would have been told that I was exempt from National Service.

※

I made my way back to what I knew would be a sad and grief stricken home. When I arrived, my Mother, little sister Grace, Grandpa, Aunt Jessie and Uncle Alex were all sitting in the living room. I was glad to see that the tears had subsided somewhat and we all hugged for a while. Uncle Alex told me that he had spoken to Charlie Roberts and that he was coming in the morning to clear out the furniture in the bottom bedroom of our house. He would take everything to temporarily storage and this would clear a space in that room for my Dad's open coffin, to be placed on trestles as per my Mother's request.

Uncle Alex went on to tell me that he would see the minister of the Bourock Parish Church tonight and arrange with him a date and time for the funeral. When this was known, a notice would be put in the "Barrhead News" to inform people of my Father's death. Many people in the town would be shocked when this word got out, for he was a well-known man there.

My Father was born in Barrhead in 1902, and at the age of 14 he left school and started work in one of the grocery stores run by the Barrhead Co-Operative. They had six stores in Barrhead and my Father had worked in all of them at one time or another, serving just about everyone in town, making himself well known. At the time of his death, he was also very active in Masonic circles, being Grand Master in Barrhead as well as being active in many other lodges in the surrounding districts.

As soon as I knew the date of my Dad's funeral, I planned to set out in my Dad's car and visit friends and family who lived out of town and with whom I had no means of communication. First on my list was my married sister Agnes who lived in a district of Glasgow with her husband Frank; Agnes worked in a bakery-tearoom called "Ferguson's" in the city center, and that was where I would contact her.

※

Boxing Day in 1950 had been a shocking and dreadful day for me and I felt relieved to retire to my bedroom that night, but the tragic events of the day came flooding back to me. At last in bed, I was free to let my emotions run their course and I wept long into the night.

※

My Father's body laid in an open casket in the cold bedroom of our house for five days; many people came to see him and much weeping took place as they looked upon him for the last time. My Mother spent many hours weeping in that room and I would often hear her cry out "Oh Jimmy, you're so cold."

The day of the funeral has remained a blur to me, but I do remember the hearse coming to our house to take the coffin to the church. A short time later a limousine came to pick up my family to take us to the church, where a service was to be held for my Father.

A large proportion of the men who filled the church were from the many Masonic Orders to which my Dad was connected. The coffin below the pulpit was surrounded by a mass of flowers.

I do not remember anything of the service, but at its conclusion, my Dads coffin together with all the flowers was carried along the long pathway from the church to the Main Street of Barrhead where the hearse was waiting. The limo with Grandpa, Frank, Uncle Alex and I was behind the hearse; it was the only vehicle that followed the hearse to the cemetery.

As the coffin and flowers were placed in the hearse, the large crowd that had gathered and filled the street, stood in silence and then lined up in threes behind our limo; there must have been at least a hundred men there.

The hearse drove at walking pace as it made its way from the church to the Neilston Cemetery, about a mile away and uphill. I remember looking back through the rear window of the limo to see that long line of men in dark suits marching in silence behind.

Again, I do not remember the graveside service except the moment when my Father's casket was lowered into the grave and my Grandfather (who was deaf) said in a loud voice "Why Jimmy? Why couldn't they have taken me.?"

After the graveside service was over, the limousine took the four of us to the Centre Cinema Cafe in Barrhead, which was the largest venue in town for private luncheon gatherings.

My Mother and sisters were there, as were my aunts, cousins and family friends, and many of our older relatives who were unable to walk to the cemetery. While we waited for the men to walk back from the cemetery, we shook hands, hugged, and made idle chatter. We were then seated at several long tables and enjoyed a three course luncheon of soup, steak- pie and trifle for dessert.

After the luncheon was over, several people stood up and talked about my Dad. The speeches did not last too long, and we finally hugged again and said our goodbyes; the funeral was over, my Dad had reached his final resting place.

It had been a grief filled six days; I was relieved and glad that it was now all behind us, and I felt a calming and more gentle feeling now take over.

※

In all the years since that sad day, I have never witnessed a funeral like the one that my Dad had. He was only forty-eight years old, and perhaps that was partly the reason for this outpouring of grief, but I believe that it was mainly the respect that people had for him as a man, that brought everyone to honour him at his end.

The Ritchie family, 10 day's before my Father died.
Agnes, Frank, Jim, Grace, Grandpa, Mum and Dad.

NATIONAL SERVICE: "TWO YEARS OF MY LIFE"

After my Dad's passing, the Ritchie family was never the same again, but life had to go on and we picked up from where we had left off. My Mother and sister Grace continued working in our family 'Greengrocer, Fruit and Flower' shop located at "The Centre" in Barrhead.

My Mother and Father had bought this shop in 1942 and from then on, my Mother, my older and younger sisters plus Mrs. Douglas, an assistant, had been running the shop under the careful guidance of my Father. He would come to the shop in the evenings after it closed, to tidy up, rearrange things, re-do the window display and collect the day's cash. He did all this after he had worked a full day as a grocer in the Co-Op. Every one of us in the family helped in the shop, and it had been part of my life since the age of 12 when I would deliver customer orders, using the wooden handcart that I had made.

This work was done after school and on Saturday mornings. I enjoyed the work and in the process I managed to make some pocket money on the tips that customers gave me.

Getting actually paid wages for doing this work for the family shop was never even discussed.

※

As for now, I continued working as a carpenter, spending most of my working days in the woodwork shop making doors, windows, cabinets and staircases. There was also the saxophone, piping, movie going and dancing (with the occasional brief romance) that took up my spare time as I waited for my call for duty in His Majesty's Forces.

TWO

Fort George

The buff coloured envelope with "On His Majesty's Service" emblazoned along the top was delivered to our house as expected. It contained a letter, and a one-way ticket to Inverness. The letter had instructions for me to report to the Regimental Headquarters of the Cameron Highlanders at Fort George on the 15th. of March 1951. While there, I would undergo sixteen weeks of intensive infantry training with the Argyll and Sutherland Highlanders Regiment, who were presently in Korea as part of the Commonwealth Brigade, and at the completion of my training, I would be joining this regiment in Korea as reinforcement.

As could be expected, my Mother got a shock when she read this letter; her husband was dead barely three months and now her son was leaving, and was being sent to a war zone at the other end of the world, to a place she had never heard of until just recently. She was visibly upset after reading this notice, but knew there was nothing she could do to prevent it. Like countless Mothers before her whose sons went off to war, it was a burden she had to bear.

The night before leaving, we had a small family gathering in our house to wish me good luck in "doing my bit" for our country. As always at these affairs it would be tea and cakes, for no alcoholic beverages were ever served or consumed in our house.

I had no idea when my first leave might be, but guessed it to be at least a couple of months, so I said I would see them all again at that time. Then it was hugs and kisses all around, and the next time they would see me I would be a full-fledged soldier.

Next morning I said goodbye to my teary-eyed Mother and carrying a small case with personal belongings and some food that my Mother had made, I was off to catch the bus to Glasgow and from there the train to Inverness. I was actually looking forward to this train trip because it would be the longest that I had ever taken, and having studied the map, I knew that it would pass through some very scenic spots on the way to Inverness.

The train was not very busy, and on my walk through the cars, I noticed that it had a very nice dining car. I suddenly felt hungry and decided to treat myself to a nice three course lunch, encouraged in this endeavour by the mouth watering aromas that were wafting around. Goodness knew when I would be able to do that again!

The dining car tables were set with white tablecloths and silver cutlery, and when the waiter came to serve me, I believe he recognized me for what I was: a young man leaving home for the first time, going off to do his National Service.

I asked him what he would suggest and he said "For two and six you can have the steak pie and all the extras." That sounded great and I ordered it and was waited on like a king. Soup, salad, fish course, then the main course; I had four servers waiting on me at once, each with a large silver container from which they served a variety of vegetables, as much as I wanted. This was followed by dessert and tea and when finished, I thought to myself, wow, what a wonderful "Last Meal". As it turned out, this would in fact to be my last good meal for many weeks to come, and I thank those waiters for realizing that, and treating me as they did.

At Inverness station a red faced sergeant was bawling: "Fort George recruits over here!" There were about ten of us on that train and we were transported to "The Fort" on a truck with a canvas top and benches inside for sitting.

It was a cold day in March as we drove to the Fort, and it was raining slightly. Inside the truck, all ten of us chatted excitedly and wondered what we were getting into. About half an hour later the truck stopped, we jumped out and my first thought was, where is the Fort? We were standing in the midst of a number of smaller wood buildings and several larger Nissen type buildings. Looking beyond those, I saw for the first time the massive stone walls of this 18th century edifice called Fort George.

※

Work began on the building of Fort George in 1746 after the Battle of Culloden, which was the final battle of the Highland Clans when they joined forces in a misguided attempt to march into England, defeat the English army, dethrone the German Monarch, King George 2nd. and crown their Prince Charlie, who claimed to be the rightful heir to the throne. The battle was a bloodbath; Highland warriors in kilts brandishing claymore's (swords) against a modern army equipped with muskets and cannons, it was no contest. The Highlanders were slaughtered and retribution against the remaining Highlanders was carried out for many years afterwards. The Battle of Culloden was fought not far from where Fort George was built.

The fort was built on a spit of land jutting into Moray Firth, just north-east of Inverness, and it was to be the ultimate defence against any further unrest in the Highlands. To this day, it remains the mightiest 18th. Century artillery fortification in Britain. Its walls measure almost a mile around, with three of its sides facing the water and the fourth side which faces the land has a moat and drawbridge. The parade ground alone is bigger than the Edinburgh Castle esplanade. It took 21 years to complete, and its 18th century bastioned defences and original garrison buildings have survived intact. Since my stint at the Fort, it has been restored, and is now a British National Historic Site.

At the beginning of the 2nd World War, in order to accommodate more men, wooden huts and ancillary buildings were erected outside, on what had been the approaches to the Fort, and it was to these huts that we were assigned lodging. This was to be my home for the next sixteen weeks.

※

On that very first day, we were fitted out with our uniforms and given most of our equipment which we had to sign and be responsible for. In the thin brown "Soldiers Record and Pay Book" that we were issued, was the chart "Sizes of Garments" which stated the size of every piece of clothing we received. Carrying the garments and equipment, we were marched to one of the huts and assigned a space containing a bed. Thirty-two recruits arrived that day, sixteen to a hut, two huts A and B. Two sergeants, a corporal and a lance corporal hustled us here and there, shouting and insulting us all the while as we continued to collect the bedding and other bits of our "kit". The mattress on the bed was made of three thin cushions called "biscuits".

Without stopping, we were marched down to the MI. (Medical) room, lined up and given a series of inoculations, then marched back to our hut and told that we would have the next day, Sunday, free.

All our civilian clothes were to be taken to the QM. (Quarter-master's) store where they would be parcel'd up and mailed to our parents. If we wanted to escape from what may turn out to be some form of tyranny, it would be very difficult since we would have to do it in uniform. We have heard stories of young men who did try to escape and were brought back to the Fort to receive some very harsh treatment from the bullying and sadistic NCO's. in charge of training. The length of time an escapee was "absent without leave " (AWOL.) was doubled, and added on to his two years' National Service. There was one particular lad whom we heard about who walked away several times and had finished up with serving three years of National Service instead of two. Judging by the way these unfortunates were treated, some of them could quite easily have ended up in a mental institution.

Back in our cold barrack room, it didn't take long before the vaccines pumped into us began to take effect. Our arms began to swell up and we became feverish. None of us felt the cold that night in that unheated wooden hut; we were burning up with fever. Next morning three of the lads had to be taken to the hospital in the Fort, suffering from delirium, while the rest of us lay in bed and suffered the pain and fever. I ate nothing since arriving at the Fort, nor I wanted any; that wonderful meal on the train kept me going.

Life in the British Army began the next morning with the arrival of the Orderly Sergeant at our hut at 6:00 a.m. This man soon took on the face of a devil god, who was to be avoided at all cost because of the punishment he could mete out. His typical behaviour in the morning was to bang the doorknob with his hand, throw the door open and yell the order "Everybody up" just before hitting the light switches.

This was still late winter and dark until 8:00 a.m. He would then go to the only stove we had in the room, pick up the poker and bang it loudly on the empty coal bucket. His next statement would be that he'll be back in five minutes and anyone not out of bed and getting dressed would be put on a charge. We soon found out that being "put on a charge" was a form of punishment that meant extra work and drills.

Typically a person on charge would present himself to the Orderly Sergeant at 5:00 a.m. in the Guard House, where he would be inspected to see if he was washed, shaved and properly dressed and if not, he could have extra time added on to his charge. He would then be taken outside and subjected to strong tongue-lashing and physical abuse, and ordered to run around the parade square with his rifle high over his head for half an hour. At 6:00 a.m. he would return to his bed with the Orderly Sergeant and it would be inspected once again, and if all was not in perfect order, more time would be added to his charge. He would then join the squad for our regular strenuous daily activity, at the end of which he would report to the Quartermaster Sergeant, the person in charge of the stores. The poor recruit would then do an extra two hours of work before going back to his barrack room to take care of his uniform and equipment for the next morning's inspection.

This extra work, stress and humiliation and resistance to this form of discipline made some of the boys crack up after a while, and they were immediately transferred out of the infantry and into another regiment like the Army Service Corps where discipline was not a prime criteria.

It should be remembered that this was still winter in the north of Scotland and it was usually frosty and very cold in the morning. The hut was like a fridge with hoar frost covering all the windows, so getting out of bed in the morning was a major feat. After the Orderly Sergeant left with his promise of returning in five minutes, nobody would stir as we listened in silence to the sound of his hob-nailed boots ringing against the concrete sidewalk as he made his way around the square, inflicting the same dire warning to the three other huts in our vicinity. He would then make his way back to our hut, and as his hand hit the doorknob, everyone in the room would leap as one, out from the cosiness of their bed and be standing at attention as the Orderly Sergeant took his first step into our hut. Some of the boys would quickly get their clothes on and head for the washhouse that stood at one end of the drill square. I was told that if one got there quick enough, there was hot water for the first few men, but in all my sixteen weeks I never had the pleasure of that luxury; it was a cold water wash and shave for me every morning. Some of the younger boys had not started shaving yet, but they shaved anyway, for to be inspected and found to have as much as a trace of fuzz on their face would mean being put on a charge.

We were drilled daily on the square, "square bashing" it was called. I had no trouble with drills because of my Boys Brigade experience, but some of the lads had problems with even the simplest of commands and would face the wrath of the Drill Sergeant who would instantly pick on them. Standing two inches from their face, screaming humiliations, calling the man a "brain dead nignog", and then scream some more.. "What did I just call you" asked the torturer? The unfortunate recruit would be required to shout out. "A brain dead nignog, Sir." Nignog was a new word for all of us new recruits and it was used constantly by our drill instructors to demean and humiliate as we learned how to instantly respond correctly to any command given. By the end of our sixteen weeks of training, we were surprised to find ourselves to be a finely drilled unit and were actually very proud of it.

That's me, front left, with my Squadies in Fort George.

During that first week of training at the Fort, the NCO's on the parade ground were keen to find someone to humiliate, someone they could make an example to shock and impress us new recruits. One morning after washing, shaving, being properly dressed and having had our barrack room inspected, we were lined up on the parade ground, standing to attention for inspection, as was normal before being marched to the mess hall for breakfast. Suddenly Corporal Calder, the meanest of all the NCO's screamed out. "What is this? What is this? This filthy man has not washed his neck; come and have a look Lance Corporal Waymire". His cohort, the Lance Corporal came running over, checked the man's neck and said. "It is absolutely filthy Sir, shall I get a bucket of water, soap and scrubbing brush?" They had obviously been through this routine before, so Corporal Calder cried out: "Right away Lance Corporal."

The three articles of cleansing appeared magically, and the unfortunate recruit was ordered to strip to the waist. This particular morning was cold and frosty, all of us were dressed in fatigues (denim uniform) and sweaters. The Lance Corporal proceeded to scrub the recruit's neck, using a large bar of soap and a stiff bristle brush. When he was finished to Corporal Calder's satisfaction, he picked up the bucket and sloshed some of the water on the unfortunate's neck and shouted: "Now this is how clean I expect all of you nignogs to be the next time I inspect you."

The discipline imposed on us was cruel, but I am sure that it had the desired effect because from that day on, there would be no unwashed necks on parade from our squad ever again!

In addition to the drilling, we had daily periods of weapons training, both in the classroom and in the field. We learned the mechanical functions of the Lee Enfield 303 rifle, the Sten gun , the Bren gun and the two- inch mortar. In the "Butts" (rifle range) we learned how to use them, and I discovered that I was a little bit color blind. In the Butts, we would fire at targets from a variety of distances up to 500 yards. These targets were made of wood and canvas, and were controlled by some of us who 'manned' the Butts in a deep, purpose built trench. The targets were made to pop up before we fired at them and then lowered so that the results could be inspected. We would then be marked according to our accuracy with the rifle.

The targets were about four feet square and painted a buff color with a large red circle in the middle and a black bulls-eye, about six inches in diameter. Looking at these target's backed by a high sand embankment caused the colors to blend together for me, and all I could see to shoot at was the black bulls-eye. This must have caused me to concentrate more on what I was shooting at, for I got good marks with the rifle, a weapon that I had never used before, or have since.

I clearly remember the first time our squad was taken to the rifle range: it was soon after our arrival at the Fort, the ground was frozen hard and there were patches of snow. It was a cold day, and all of us were ordered to wear our newly issued greatcoats. So there I was, lying on the ground in the snow, adjusting the rangefinder on my rifle to the distance that I was firing from, my hands and feet numb with the cold, and I was about to take my first shot with a rifle. We had been told to hold the rifle tightly against our right shoulder as there would be quite a kick from it when we pulled the trigger. I thought I was doing everything correctly, but when I pulled the trigger, the kick was so much greater than expected that my left hand, which was holding the front of the rifle, came back with such force that I punched myself on the nose and it started to bleed. That was a low point for me; there was my blood in the snow, I was freezing cold and I lay there wondering with dismay how I was ever going to survive sixteen weeks of this hell.

Some of my squadies and I taken a break; you can see the walls of the "Fort" behind.

Hand grenades; how they work and how to use them was also part of our training. In the classroom, we were introduced to the hand grenade, which looks like a small pineapple. It is packed with explosives and when it explodes, it sends a shower of small pieces of metal in all directions, killing or wounding anyone who gets in the way. To detonate a hand grenade, you pull a metal ring that is attached to a pin; when the pin comes out you have five seconds to get rid of the grenade before it explodes. It is a dangerous weapon to have around and some of the lads were afraid even to hold a live one in their hands.

We practiced with dummy grenades before going to the grenade grounds to do the real thing. The grenade ground was well away from every other facility in Fort George. It consisted of a deep, curving trench that led to a forward trench that was a couple of steps higher up. This was called the fighting bench, because you could see over to a large level piece of ground where we would throw our grenades. At the other end of this trench was a large underground bunker with benches. This bunker, made of old creosoted railroad ties, with its flat roof covered with about three feet of soil, was well camouflaged.

The drill at the grenade ground was for all of our squad to go into the bunker and wait in line. Of the first two men to go out, one would go to the fighting bench where a junior officer would oversee the throw, and the other would wait in line below him in the trench, so that only two men would be out of the bunker at one time. If any of the grenades thrown failed to explode, the officer in charge and a munitions expert would walk out, identify the grenade, put an explosive charge beside it, walk back to the trench and then detonate it from there. The squad had been at the grenade ground before and had witnessed these events, but this time it would be much different.

Ready for more drilling on the Square.

Two days before our second trip to the grenade ground, our sergeant had been lecturing us about an explosive material called "guncotton". He showed us what it looked like; it was about the size of a large bar of soap, grey in color and hard as cement. It looked harmless, and it was, until detonated by a special timed detonator that could be set for as long as required before exploding. The sergeant stressed that the explosive force was always upward, and never downward; he was wrong there.

Unknown to us, at our next visit to the grenade grounds he planned to make the battle scene more realistic by exploding some guncotton over our bunker.

So here we were in the bunker, the first two men had finished their throw and returned. My companion and I were next out; he was in the fighting bench getting ready to throw his grenade, and I was in the trench behind him waiting my turn. There was a loud explosion behind me and I could see dirt and pieces of wood flying in the air, then a second later I heard shrieks and yells coming from the bunker that I had just left. I rushed back to see the smoking remains of where an explosion had just occurred; it was just over the opening to the bunker, its wood framing now shattered. The sergeant was there just ahead of me, and was already in the bunker talking to two of my squadies who were injured by flying chunks of wood from the shattered roof.

They both had to go to the hospital to get their arms patched up and were excused from duty for the next four days. The sergeant was court-marshalled for committing actions endangering his men, but was absolved two days later and was back as one of the NCO's putting us through our paces.

The squad had been locked away in Fort George, (confined to barracks). for over eight weeks, and we were wondering if we would ever get to leave this place of misery. When the joyous news came out that the squad after ten weeks of training would be granted four days of leave, we were overjoyed. We would be issued a pass that we could show to any Military Police who would stop us, and they certainly did: for every railway station was swarming with M.P.'s on the lookout for deserters, for young men who had had enough of the Army and were trying to escape. To be truthful, the thought of doing just that had crossed my mind several times.

I headed for home, and the four days were sheer bliss; sleeping in my own bed and my Mother spoiling me.

Just about all my friends were gone, doing their National Service like myself, so I was mostly alone and spent the time loafing around, working in the garden and going to the movies. This was a kind of an aimless existence that I was no longer used to, and strangely enough I began to look forward to getting back to Fort George to be with my squadies again.

From then on, life at the Fort seemed a little less strict, the tongue lashing and abuse from the NCO's a little less severe. The result no doubt of having been indoctrinated into Army life, and of getting used to being shoved around.

Concentration on physical conditioning of our squad was perhaps greater than on other training. Taking long runs, strenuous workouts in the large gymnasium, weekly assaults of the obstacle course, which I rather enjoyed, but it was here where some of the men who "could not cut the mustard" were weeded out and transferred to some other branch of the Army. Then there were the route marches of up to ten miles, with a heavy pack and carrying a rifle. Spartan living and weeks of strenuous outdoor exercise brought us to peak physical condition, to a state where we felt indestructible and capable of doing any task requested or desired.

In the evenings, we cleaned our gear, polished our boots and brasses, then pressed any part of our uniform that was wrinkled to be ready for the next days inspection. After finishing chores, we would organize a wrestling match; one end of the hut against the other. Mattresses would be laid out in the middle of the hut and we would all wrestle for two hours or so. Not once in all the weeks there had any boy have a grudge against any other. We had built up a wonderful loyalty to each other, even though we smiled inwardly when someone was picked on, or given harsh treatment by those NCO bullies. We were glad it was not us, and afterwards in our hut we would all have a real good belly laugh when the comic of our group, "Fog" Robertson would re-enact a recent "dressing down" that one of us had just had, by impersonating the antics of the Sergeant or his cohort prig Lance Corporal Waymire.

At other times, in a burst of exuberance and vitality that is reserved strictly for the young, we would go down to the gymnasium and simply work our way around it, climb the wall bars or the ropes. There was also a good vaulting horse there that we made good use in our eagerness to unload some built up energy. Here my Boy's Brigade training came useful, for I was able to show the boys how to do vaulting on the horse.

My undoing came when demonstrating how to do a neck spring off the horse. In this exercise you run up, spring on the springboard and land on the horse, with your hands taking the weight and your forehead planted, head and arms forming a triangle. You hold this position fractionally with legs in the air parallel to the horse, then spring off, and land on your feet. On one of these demonstrations my feet got tangled up and I made a bad landing; my left foot got caught under me and I came down on it, wrenching it pretty badly. It immediately swelled up like a balloon and felt like something was broken. For a few moments the boys gathered around to look at my foot and give me their sympathies, then carried on with their own workouts and I was left to my resources.

I immediately dunked my foot in a nearby fire-bucket that was filled with water; it eased the pain slightly, but after a few minutes I decided to hop back to the hut and lie down on my bed. Ten minutes of hopping got me back to the hut and I was soon stretched out on my back with my eyes closed, contemplating my fate. As usual, some of the boys in the hut were wrestling and my contemplation came to an abrupt end when two of the wrestlers landed on top of me, and more specifically on my injured foot. The searing pain and nausea that accompanies such an assault on the system had barely subsided when our beloved Corporal Calder came into the hut and ordered everyone to be out in the square at 4:00 a.m. and be properly dressed for night manoeuvres. He took one look at my foot and said: "You report sick to the Medical. Room at 7:00 a.m."

Reporting sick was not an easy task, made as difficult as possible to prevent it from abuse by those who would feign sickness to escape duties or the rigours of training.

At 4:00 a.m. the hut was cleared and the boys were out in the square properly dressed, their faces smeared with black cream as required, and I was left on my own to report sick. To do this, I had to make up a small pack including a change of underwear, pyjamas, towel, toilet kit, socks, gym outfit and gym shoes. The rest of my gear was to be packed into a large wooden chest we were all issued. This, together with my blankets, pillow, greatcoat and rifle were to be turned in to the Quarter-Master Sergeant and signed for at 6:00 a.m. The QM stores were about 200 yds. from our hut and it took me two hours and several trips to get everything there, because I could only use one foot, while the other was a throbbing stump. It meant hopping on one foot and dragging the chest, then back and forth for the other items.

At 6:00 a.m. everything was checked in and all I had to carry was my greatcoat and small pack as I made my way to the Medical Room, another 300 yds. away. Shortly after 7:00 a.m. I was admitted to the MO's (Medical Officer) office. After a quick examination of my foot, he told me to report to the hospital in the Fort, a distance of about half a mile. When I asked about transportation, he told me to make my own way there. With all the hopping on my good leg earlier in the morning, it was now cramping up and about as sore as the damaged foot. With the Old Soldiers

Motto "Ours is not to reason why, ours is but to do and die" ringing in my ears, I set off on the long journey, grateful for being physically fit for the task ahead.

I arrived at the Fort Hospital, lathered in sweat and in a state of near exhaustion with my greatcoat neatly folded over my arm. I was put in a bed right away and my foot examined. It was decided that nothing was to be done as no break was detected (no x-rays were taken). A large cage was installed over the foot of the bed to keep the weight of the blankets off my feet, and I was left there to heal.

Sheer exhaustion and the comfort of the bed made me fall into a deep sleep from which I awoke only next morning when breakfast was brought to me in bed – what a luxury! I stayed in bed for the next five days, enjoying the pleasures of just eating, sleeping and reading. The MO would come daily to make his inspections, during which we were expected to sit at attention and look straight ahead.

After five days, the MO told me that if I felt like it, I could get up. I didn't feel like it and continued to stay in bed until the bossy and strict head nurse came by, and giving me her sternest look, she uttered one word: "Up!"

There was no use arguing with her, and as I made my move she said: "I want you up and moving around." The fact that my foot was still very swollen and painful, making it difficult to put any weight on it made no impression on her.

The next day I received the news that I would be put to work, and my job would be polishing the floors in the hospital. To do this I, was given a contraption made up of a heavy, cast iron plate to which a thick felt pad was attached, and all that on a pivoting broom handle; a kind of crude floor polisher. I would first have to give the portion of the floor to be polished a coat of wax applied by hand and then using this buffer, bring it to a high shine. Part of this job I could do on my hands and knees, but the buffing could only be done standing up and hopping on my one good leg. My so-called "soft touch" in the hospital came to an end.

Meanwhile the squad's activities were going right ahead, and every evening one or two of the boys would come in to see me and bring me up to date with what was happening. My greatest fear was of being "back- squadded", that is being assigned into the next squad that was recruited two weeks after us; such was the loyalty that had built up among us.

After seven days of polishing the floors, I was desperate to get out of there, and even though I could hardly put weight on my foot, I told the MO that I was fine and he discharged me the next day back to my old squad.

It was with great difficulty that I squeezed my army boot over my still swollen foot, but it did provide some support, and as time went on, the pain lessened. But my foot remained swollen for many months, and gave me trouble for even years afterwards. The tightly laced boot gave me support on the Parade Ground, but it was the end of my visits to the gym.

Fortunately for me, a lot of our training was now in classroom lectures, learning what would be expected of us when we joined our regiment at the end of our sixteen weeks training We were also shown some very graphic pictures of what would happen if we were foolish enough to engage in sexual activities while abroad, resulting in venereal disease.

At one of our final lectures we learned that at the completion of our training, we would leave Fort George taking all our kit except rifles, and enjoy a fourteen day embarkation leave. At the end of this leave, we would take a train to Liverpool with a rail pass provided, and on arrival, we would be re-issued with our rifles. Fully equipped, we would next board a troopship to Hong Kong for a further ten weeks of training before shipping to Korea to join our regiment, the Argyll and Sutherland Highlanders. It was nice to know finally what was planned for us.

This was our squad half way through our training. I am in the back row six from the left, our barrack room is behind us.

Our basic training came to an end with a flurry of night exercises, full-kit route marches and several full-kit inspections, when all our kit had to be displayed on our bed in a prescribed fashion. Every item in our kit had to be scrupulously clean, polished and pressed, and the arrangement of all in that prescribed fashion took some time to do. Most of us worked on laying out our kit on the bed the night before, and slept on the floor in order to avoid getting up an hour early to get it done before the inspection.

The squad's final hurrah to Fort George was the RSM's (Regimental Sergeant Major) parade, which happened to coincide with our "Passing Out Parade."

The RSM's parade was held on the main square, attended by all troops stationed in the Fort, upwards of seven hundred men from the Argyll, Seaforth, Cameron, Black Watch and Gordon Highlanders, all in the full dress-uniform of their regiment. In our case, it was the Argyll and Sutherland

Highlanders, and we dressed accordingly in the Campbell tartan kilts.

Our squad was reduced to sixteen members by then; we were the final survivors of the original thirty-two. A pipe band attended this event, and as we were the only squad to be "passing out" that day, we had the honour of marching past the rest of the troops while the pipe band played for us. This was a proud moment for our squad. We all felt a great sense of achievement and we marched with precision, heads held high, and with the pipes playing we felt a great sense of patriotism flooding through us. We had made it!

It was without regrets that we left the cold grey stone walls of Fort George for the last time. It might have been easier for us had we spent our sixteen weeks of training housed in its historic barrack rooms.

On one of my few trips around the Fort, I was warned to always walk quickly and smartly, and never walk across the parade and drill square in the centre, for to step on it when not part of a parade or squad, would mean being put on instant charge. The only way to get to the other side of that square was to walk around it.

I visited Fort George many years later on a nostalgic trip; by then it was declared a National Historic Site, and had been extensively restored to its original 18th Century condition. The wood buildings where I did my training, and all the others that were cluttered around inside the Fort were all gone.

Jim ready for the R.S.M.'s Parade.

THREE

Troopship to Afar

After checking through the MP's at Inverness Station, our squad boarded the train for Glasgow, fully laden with our kit and looking forward to fourteen days of glorious leave. I was now able to look back on what I often call the most miserable sixteen weeks of my life. We all had a one way train ticket from Glasgow to Liverpool and we planned to meet again when our leave was over to talk about how much we enjoyed ourselves on our leave.

It was the ultimate luxury to be back home in my own bed again, even though I had to sleep in the same room with my Grandpa who snored loudly. My Mother waited on me like a king, with breakfast in bed and special dinners.

I found out that one of my good friends, Jim Anderson, was also home on leave for two weeks; he was heading for either Cyprus or the Canal Zone after his leave. We would be good company during our leave, and we intended to catch up on all the dancing and pretty girls that we had been missing out on for the past many weeks.

I had my Dad's car at my disposal, so on our first Saturday night, we headed to Largs,, a small town on the Ayrshire coast, with a beautiful ballroom called "The Moorings". We knew it would be full of the prettiest girls imaginable, and we were not disappointed, for while there we met and danced with two of these very pretty girls from Paisley, who had come to Largs by train, and would soon have to leave the dancehall to catch the train back home.

In those days, not many young men had cars, so here was my big chance to impress these two young ladies, and I asked "How would you feel about Jimmy and I taking you home to Paisley in my car?" I guess they felt there was safety in numbers, because they readily agreed and we all had a wonderful time driving back to Paisley singing all the way. From then on Jean Campbell was my date, and Joyce was Jimmy's. The girls were working, but Jimmy and I had the evenings and weekends to take them dancing, movies and just driving around, visiting some of the scenic spots not far from Barrhead and Paisley. Jean promised to write me when I was away, and Joyce to Jimmy, and they did as promised.

It seemed like in no time my leave was coming to an end, and the evening before I left we had a bit of a bon voyage party at home (tea and cakes). There was my Mother, Grandpa (the last time I would see him), my younger sister Grace, my older sister Agnes and her husband Frank, my Aunt Jessie and Uncle Alex, and finally my dog Sheila, who would also die before I returned. They all promised to write, and so did I. No tears were shed and I felt like I was going away on a two weeks' holiday, but it would be eighteen months before I returned home again.

The last thing my Mother said to me next morning as I left home for Glasgow was "Come back home safe Jim!" and off I went.

※

As I have mentioned before, every bus depot and train station was watched closely by Military Police, and any unfortunate soldier who missed his train or whose pass expired before the next train left, would be deemed to be AWOL. He would be arrested by the MP's and taken to a military jail where he could expect some unpleasant confinement before being shipped back to his regiment for sentencing. Consequently, very few soldiers ever missed that all-important connection.

In Liverpool our train was met by the MP's who hustled us onto trucks and we were driven to the docks where we were united with the rest of our squad. In a large shed, an officer from the Shropshire Light Infantry briefed us with the news that we had been assigned to his regiment for the duration of the voyage. Then he went on with what we already knew about the voyage taking six weeks, and that we would undergo a further ten weeks training in Hong Kong before leaving for Korea.

※

The name of our troopship was HMS Devonshire and it would be taking several thousand men to Hong Kong and ports in between where the British Army was operating. We boarded the vessel with all our gear and were directed immediately to our deck assignment on the lowest deck. This assignment was not unexpected, for we had no officer to speak for us, and the infantry, especially the National Service, were expected to tough it out more than anyone else.

We occupied a corner of this deck, at the lowest point at the stern of the ship. The deck area was very spacious and had long tables coming out at right angles from the side of the ship with benches attached, and were ranged down both sides of the deck. Each table seated sixteen, eight on each side, perfect for our squad. The centre of the deck was open, except for some large storage space where our hammocks and kit was stowed. Our "lodgings" looked pretty good to be our home for the next six weeks.

By next evening the ship was fully loaded and at high tide, we cast off with the aid of two tugs, and sailed down the Mersey Channel into the Irish Sea. Most of us were on deck watching the land slip past. A mist was settling on the river and it seemed to match our melancholy mood as we wondered if we would ever see this land again or be buried in some foreign grave. It was August 1st 1951.

In a remarkably short time ,we settled into the routine of the ship. Our first major task was to master the art of sleeping in a hammock, which we slung up in the open area of the deck in the evening. No more sleeping on stomachs or sides; from then on we all slept on our backs and slept wonderfully well. Our squad was still as active and full of fun as ever, so we took turns at annoying each other by slipping out of our hammocks when we thought everyone was asleep, creep under the sleeping men and selecting one to heave up from below to dump the sleeping occupant onto the deck. Surprisingly, no one ever got hurt with this prank; with our youthfully quick reactions we would all land cat-like on our feet.

Reveille was at 7:00 a.m.; we were washed, shaved, properly dressed and inspected at 7:45 a.m. when four men were assigned for duty that day. They would then report to the galley for food for our table. After eating, they would fetch a large tub of hot water to wash our dishes and utensils. Everyone except those on duty would then leave the table and the duty squad would be responsible for the washing up and drying and the return of dishes to the galley. The duty squad would then scrub the tabletop, benches, the deck under the table and the open deck area. An inspection was made at the completion of this work taking about an hour, and then the rest of us were free to come back and get ready for whatever activities had been planned for that day. These activities were mainly physical and weapons training and inspections. We had lectures on personal hygiene with emphasis on venereal diseases and the need to be fastidious if we wanted to avoid things like Tropical Impetigo, Prickly Heat, athlete's foot and several other nastiness.

The weather was good and the sea calm as we crossed the dreaded Bay of Biscay, dreaded because we all heard about the storms that could brew up there, and because none of us had ever been on a long sea voyage. Talking about seasickness was a popular topic of conversation.

The first land we sighted was the famous Rock of Gibraltar as the ship sailed east through the well known Straits. We were entering the Mediterranean and for me, and likely for most of the men on the ship, this voyage was a revelation, an opening of my consciousness about the rest of the world, a world that had only existed in print or on a movie screen to this time in my life.

It was exciting to watch dolphins and flying fish swim alongside us, always keeping up with the ship. Apart from the stretch through the Suez Canal, dolphins were with us all the way to Hong Kong.

The warm, salty breezes of the Med were very pleasant, and most afternoons were spent on the deck sunbathing. The rigours of our sixteen weeks' training were forgotten as we enjoyed this lovely cruise.

The ship stopped at Malta to take on water and supplies. Nobody was allowed off the ship, but we did get a good view of the harbour; the old stone fortifications that were a stopping-off point for the Crusaders many hundreds of years ago. Malta was a British Protectorate and as such, it was bombed heavily during the war that had just recently ended. The Maltese people had survived by sheltering in the great natural caves that are common throughout the island.

A British naval patrol boat came alongside to ferry ashore some important people. The patrol boat was in impeccable condition with brightly shining brass work, fresh paint and whitened ropes. As it came alongside, the Marines on board in their immaculate white, starched uniforms did a drill with their boat hooks, which was very impressive.

The British presence was evident in every port we called at, and we were shown this same display of discipline and training every time. All of us watching felt a sense of pride and patriotism, and we were very proud of our British heritage.

The Med seems like a small body of water on the map, but it took us a surprisingly long time to sail through it. One morning it was announced that a concert would be held on deck and anyone who could perform was invited to participate. The main attraction was to be the dance band of the Shropshire Light Infantry Military Band.

Watching the dolphins.

The concert was a great success, and apart from the great band that played all the popular tunes of the day, where we all had a great sing- a-long, we also had some turns by some of the soldiers on board. There were a couple of comedians keeping us in stitches with their antics, and a hypnotist who did some fantastic tricks.

There was a part of his act where he had two young men from the audience hypnotized and doing all sorts of silly things making us laugh. Then he told them that coming out of his spell they would remember nothing, go back to their seats and the concert would go on as before. But when he shouted the word "Peanuts", they would jump up and be selling newspapers on a street corner of London.

The audience was asked to keep quiet and say nothing when the two men were brought out of his spell, which he did by snapping his fingers. The men returned to their seats, seemingly unaware they had even been under a spell.

The show carried on and I was speaking to one of the young man now sitting beside me, claiming that he had never ever seen this hypnotist before, when a voice (the hypnotist's) from the audience called out "Peanuts". I could not believe the change that came over him; he was instantly hypnotized again, jumped up and started shouting "Newspaper, Newspaper, Read all about it!"

The audience roared with laughter and he seemed to slowly come out of his trance, then came back to sit beside me and said "I don't know what made me do that."

I have been mystified ever since.

※

The weather got increasingly warmer and we were allowed to sleep on deck if wished. Just a couple of blankets and a pillow on the deck, the hard opposite to sleeping in a hammock. This was another first for me, sleeping out in the open under a canopy of stars.

The next port of call was Port Said at the mouth of the Suez Canal. Once again no one was allowed off the ship; at that time Egypt was hot with nationalistic fever under its strong man dictator Abdul Nasser, who wanted to nationalize the Suez Canal, then under the control of Britain and France.

Our troopship left Port Said just as the sun was going down, and as we slowly sailed into position to enter the canal, we passed what was my first look at a cruise ship, tied up at one of the docks and lit up like a Christmas tree. A dance band was playing softly in the ship's ballroom, which was on the top deck open on all sides, and we had a wonderful view of the dancers as they swirled around. As we slowly sailed past, many of dancers came out to the side of their ship to wave. The ladies were dressed in long evening gowns and the men in tuxes or tails, all holding cocktail glasses, looking colourful, happy and well fed. Seeing them, I suddenly felt like the poor relative, the male version of a Cinderella, when everything in my life seemed suddenly drab. Listening to the wonderful music the dance band was playing made me feel a bit melancholy, and I promised myself that one day I would be one of those passengers on a luxury liner with a cocktail glass in hand. It would be twenty-three years before I fulfilled that promise.

As we sailed through the canal next day, the anti-British sentiment was evidenced by people standing on the banks, waving a clenched fist at our ship. Into the Red Sea we sailed, and the temperature rose steadily as we crossed the Tropic of Cancer. All this heat was just wonderful, and we took full advantage of it by lying out on the deck sunbathing every afternoon, and soon all of us were sporting a healthy tan.

One day I went up to a very crowded deck and found a place to lie down near the prow of the ship. The soft tropical breeze and the moist sea air brought me an overwhelming sense of contentedness and I dropped off into deep sleep, which was quite unusual for me. I awakened some time later and had no idea how long I was asleep. The once crowded deck was now completely empty; I was all alone, as the intense heat had driven everyone else below deck. I arose rather groggily and staggered along the deck to get down below as well. It was then that I noticed that from where I was lying on the deck, my sweat had created a small rivulet about twenty feet long! I must have been close to becoming dehydrated, and I wondered at the time how much water the human body contains.

To cool down I went directly to the showers, knowing that there were no fresh water showers on board and I would have to be content with a salt-water shower, where a special soap was needed to get any sort of lather. The shower cooled me down and I am sure that my body sucked in a quart of water to rehydrate itself. The only thing wrong with salt-water showers is that you never felt clean afterwards; the skin was sticky with salt.

Fresh water was almost non-existent on the HMS Devonshire. No one ever used the drinking fountain on board because the water tasted foul. The water in this fountain was warm distilled seawater with some chemical added for good measure. Our main source of liquids was from large mugs of tea available at every meal, and there was also a "Tiffin" break every afternoon when tea would be available on deck.

The food on board was always very good and tasty; the portions were satisfactory which is not always easy to measure when serving young healthy men who are always hungry. At the evening meals, the young officer from the Shropshire's who had been assigned our squad for the duration of our voyage, enquired if everything was satisfactory. No one ever complained about anything; we enjoyed this free world cruise to the fullest.

This officer was also inspecting us every morning before breakfast, and he would later oversee us engaged in rifle practice to a target towed from the back of the ship. The target could be pulled back to the ship so that we could check our firing accuracy. This area of the ship was very busy every morning as the Shropshire regiment was also on the way to Korea.

Down we sailed to the south end of the Red Sea, through the Bab-el-Mandeb Straits and into the Port of Aden for more water and supplies. At that time, Aden was a British Protectorate, but a very poor Arab state. Oil had not yet been discovered there, an event, which would later have a tremendous impact on this poverty-stricken country. Some of the men on the ship were to be allowed ashore, and we drew names to determine who the lucky ones were going to be. None of us had been off the ship since leaving Liverpool, so the desire in our squad to step ashore was great, and we were overjoyed when we were fortunate enough to have been picked.

Jungle green uniform.

Stepping ashore in Aden was like stepping back into the pages of the Bible. It seemed to be populated by men and small boys only, with the occasional heavily veiled woman blending into the background. The streets were narrow and dusty, with goats and chickens roaming freely. The buildings were plastered one and two story structures, some with verandas in front. There were some date palm trees and small bushes here and there, so that it was pleasant and colourful to walk along the short thoroughfare and take in the sights, sounds and smells of this ancient city. One building in particular I remember well, it looked like a general store with a covered patio area in front that had tables and chairs.

There was a big sign in front that advertised "Iced Fruit Drinks". The two other fellows I was with and myself were suddenly consumed with a great thirst, so in we went, sat down and ordered ourselves a large one. It had now been over three weeks since anything remotely cold had passed over our lips, and here we were, sitting in one of the hottest places on earth, drooling over what was about to be served up.

Three large drinks were brought to us with broken ice floating on top. If I live to be a hundred, I will never taste a more delicious and satisfying drink than that one was. It was probably only water, ice and Coolade, but we talked about and drooled over that drink for many weeks afterwards.

The ship made two more stops before the end of the voyage, one at the Port of Colombo on Ceylon, and the other at Singapore. All the troops on board were allowed ashore to see the sights, to walk along the broad boulevards of Colombo with heavily laden banana trees framing the ocean. Then, looking for bargains in the busy market places of Singapore, and we felt like seasoned world travellers when reaching Hong Kong, six weeks after leaving Liverpool.

FOUR

Good luck in Hong Kong

Sailing into that wonderful harbour, that colonial outpost of the British Empire; what romantic images were conjured up in our minds as we watched ancient red-sailed Chinese junks sailing with the breeze alongside merchant ships from many nations that used Hong Kong as their main trading port.

The strip of water separating the island of Hong Kong from the mainland is perhaps a mile in width. On the island side is the city of Victoria, and in 1951 the tallest building there was the Hong Kong Bank, which was also called the Shanghai Bank. It was a twenty storey Art Deco style building that had been finished before the war, and it stood out tall against the predominately four to six storey buildings that lined the waterfront. The Japanese had occupied Hong Kong during the war and had committed many atrocities there which we would later hear about, but fortunately there had been no shelling or bombing of the city, so there was no damage to be seen.

Across the water from Victoria is the city of Kowloon on the Chinese mainland; both of these cities have wonderful deep water harbours and docks. HMS Devonshire pulled into one that was right beside the main waterfront road in Kowloon. On the dock was a military band from one of the many British regiments stationed in Hong Kong. During the six-weeks' voyage we had only heard music played on two occasions, once from the cruise ship at Suez and the other time when the band of the Shropshire played at the concert on board. This time I found the music this wonderful band was playing to be very uplifting and inspiring. All of us in the squad were very excited and in good spirits; anxious to get our feet on to dry land again.

We were kept waiting on deck for some time with our equipment by our side ready to disembark, but as usual, because we were the lowly pink faced (although by now we all had a good tan) National Servicemen, we were kept waiting, and in fact we were close to be the last men off the ship. The band kept playing, and having been a member of a band myself, I knew that all band members love to play their instruments, even when there is no one around to listen to them. So we were pleasantly entertained during that long wait and the time passed quickly, but eventually we were ordered to strap on our equipment, pick up our kit bags and make our way to the gangplank. I had seen many pictures of troops coming down the gangplank of a ship with their kit bags slung over their shoulders, so I felt like I had been part of this scene before.

Dry land at last, and there to meet us was a weather-beaten faced sergeant from the Argyll and Sutherland Highlanders, our own regiment. There was no welcoming greeting from him, like "Welcome to Hong Kong lads", instead it was "Argyll's fall in over here, and be quick about it." When we were lined up, he told us that the Argyll's had been relieved from duty in Korea (this had happened during our six week voyage) and were now stationed in the New Territories close to the border with China. We found out later that the New Territories was a large piece of land within a thirty-mile radius of Kowloon that had been ceded to the British in 1892 during their colonial adventures. The total area of the New Territories was about 350 square miles.

When we heard the news about our regiment having been relieved from duty in Korea, we all looked at one another and thought "Great, we won't have to go to Korea now." The sergeant told us he would be marching us up the street a short distance to the Kowloon Canton Railway Station, where we would board a train to take us to the village of Fanling, about fifteen miles away, which was close to where the regiment was now barracked.

Off we marched, boarded the train, which happened to be waiting in the station , and we were soon on our way to what we thought would be the final leg of our long journey. The train was a steam engined, probably built in Glasgow, the carriages had wooden seats and the toilet was merely a section of one of the carriages partitioned off with a hole in the floor, through which you could see the ground below whizzing by. There were no hand rails or supports to hold on to, you merely had to squat over the hole, a skill that Orientals have no trouble with, but westerners have a great deal of trouble with. Needless to say, the toilet was avoided at all costs.

Fanling station reached, there was a truck to take us and our gear to the barracks. The sergeant sat in front with the driver and the rest of us got in the back with all our stuff. There were no seats in the truck, so we just had to hang on as best we could for the one mile drive to the camp. It was mid September with a temperature of about 90 degrees, and as we were dressed in our usual British Army khaki uniforms, we were feeling the heat, so the ride in the back of the truck felt pretty good with the wind blowing.

An army camp can be a very busy place, with upwards of a thousand men on hand. When we arrived, there were squads of men marching about, with many more out in a playing field doing physical training. We were taken to a typical army Nissen type hut and told that this would be our quarters. The sergeant told us to pick a bed, deposit our gear and get back out on parade in fifteen minutes. On parade meant that we would be getting inspected, which in turn meant that our boots and brasses would have to be polished and everything else about our uniform correct, or you guessed it, charges would be laid.

After inspection, we were marched down to the Adjutant's office and stood at attention while the Adjutant addressed us. He was a tall thin man about forty-five years old with a tobacco stained moustache; he spoke in a high accentuated voice and told us that as we were all National Servicemen (conscripts) we had no real or imagined affiliation with any particular regiment. Just because we had trained as Argyll's did not make us Argyll's.

This was news to us; remembering all those proud moments at our Passing Out Parade. He went on to say that because we had had it so easy on the troopship, there would be a week of intensive physical exercise to toughen us up, and then we would each be assigned to one of the Battalion Companies to complete our ten weeks of training, after which we would finally be fully acclimatized and toughened up. Then at the end of this training, we would be transferred into the Regiment of the Kings Own Scottish Borderers that had relieved the Argyll's in Korea and will then be shipped directly to Korea to join the regiment on the front line.

Hearing all this from that tall, weedy looking man was a bit of a downer and shattered our earlier optimism of having escaped going to the front. The gods would now decide our fate in battle, if in fact we ever did go into battle. We then marched back to our billets and spent the rest of the day collecting bedding, blankets and light-weight tropical uniforms. We were told that training would begin next morning at 6:00 hours, when we would be on parade for inspection, washed, shaved and in "bareskin" order (gym shorts, socks and runners).

This was our routine for seven days; the first morning a one mile run, the next day a little longer and by the end of the week seven miles. Every morning after the run we would wash up, get changed and be on parade again when we would be marched down to the dining hall for breakfast. The dining hall was a large Nissen type building with ceiling fans going constantly to try to keep the building cool, but with little effect.

The food was good and plentiful, but with all this exercise and fresh air, anything would have tasted good. The days were taken up with more physical training, lectures and weapons drill. Because the weather there is almost tropical; by noon it was close to 90 degrees. The time between one and two p.m. was "the quiet hour" when everyone was to rest and keep out of the heat. During this respite we were told to write home to our parents or sweethearts; all sixteen of us were between the ages if 18 and 20, and a few had girls to write home to, but most didn't. As I already mentioned, I had met a girl called Jean Campbell while on embarkation leave, and she would write to me occasionally, but most of my letters were to my Mother and two sisters.

The week's intensive training was over, praise the Lord, and we were once again on parade, and our ever present sergeant was actually praising our fitness. He told us that the squad was now going to be broken up and we would be sent to different companies in the battalion to continue our training. It was then that he asked this fateful question: "Can any of you play the bagpipes?"

Now it seems that some inconsequential skill that we learn in life sometimes directs the path in our life. This was one of those moments when a skill that I had learned at an early age was about to change my life in a positive and pleasant way. I could not believe that he had asked such a question, but I jumped quickly to attention and roared "Sir!" He glared at me and I fully expected him to ask some more questions but he just said "OK Private Ritchie, the Pipe Major would like to speak to you." And so it was that I shortly presented myself to Mr. Patrick McGlin, the Pipe Major of the Argyll and Sutherland Highlanders.

He was a short wiry man of about 35 years of age, and the most striking thing about him was his handsome waxed moustache. I quickly figured out that he was a man who seldom smiled, and liked to bark orders at new young recruits like myself.

I should explain a little about the hierarchy that exists in the British Army. It is arranged in levels of snobbery, similar to which existed in Victorian society during the nineteenth century. There was the poor, then the working class, followed by the middle class, the upper class and finally the gentry. All these classes functioned independently from each other, and it was very difficult to move up a class. People talked to, entertained, married into and ate with their own class. The British Army was founded on these same class distinctions. The privates socialize, eat, drink and tell jokes with one another; as soon as one of them is promoted to Corporal, he finds himself in a no-man's land. His old friends tend to restrain themselves in his presence, he finds himself alienated and is forced to find friends at his own level, which would be other corporals. Similarly with Sergeants and so on up the ranks of the non-commissioned officer. When we come to the commissioned officers, this separation of class distinction becomes more pronounced. An officer, when he speaks to you, (which is very seldom) you are not allowed to answer unless it is a direct question. Normally he will go through the sergeant or corporal who is in charge of the parade to voice any complaints that he has against you.

So it was, when I had my interview with "Pipey". (the nick-name that the Pipe Major had) He asked the questions and I answered as briefly as possible, there was no friendly banter or chitchat, and I stood at attention during the whole interview. When the interview was over, he handed me a set of pipes and told me to play a March, Strathspey and Reel, which I managed to do. When I finished, I lowered my pipes and stood at attention. He gave me his best steely look and said " OK Private Ritchie, put the pipes over there on that table and come back before me." I did as ordered and stood at attention once more. He gave me the same look and said. "Ritchie , I think you will do; report to Sergeant Pitkethly for further instructions, that is all." I roared out "Sir!" made an about- turn, brought my right foot down with a crash and then marched smartly out of his office.

So there it was; what a stroke of luck; I was now in the pipe band of the Argyll's! I went directly to the quarters of the pipe band which I found to be a step up from where I was presently quartered. All the band members were there as I walked in, and I was pleasantly surprised at how friendly they all were, especially Andy. Everyone shook my hand and welcomed me into their midst. I thought what a break, this is perhaps the "cushy" job I was dreaming about. I am going to enjoy this, piping all day, no more route marches, squad drilling or weapons training, just having a wonderful musical experience with these happy fellows. I was separated from my old squad now, part of the band, so I wouldn't be hauling off to Korea; I would complete the rest of my National Service here, and then go home. It was a lovely thought but it didn't quite work out that way.

When I got back to my old quarters, the boys just couldn't believe when I told them I was now enlisted as a member of the pipe band. Oh how they wished that they could play the pipes!

I joined with all my squadies to pack our gear, as everyone was leaving to join the Company they had been assigned to. The squad that had been together since that first day in Fort George was now being broken up. I said goodbye to them all and promised to get together with them soon.

Bob Morrison, and I at "The Peak" in Hong Kong.

All the members of the pipe band were regular soldiers; I was the only one who was a National Serviceman, and all of them had just come back from a tour of duty in Korea, where there was very little, if any, pipe playing. They were all very good pipers but had grown a bit rusty and were in the process of getting back into shape. I was fortunate here, for I was able to blend into the band easily as I knew many of the tunes. Sergeant Pitkethly "Andy" gave me the music for the tunes that the band was presently playing and told me to learn the ones that I did not know. This was a pleasant task indeed.

A typical day in the band would look something like this. Reveille at 0630 hours when we would be awakened by the bugler, who would be followed by the piper playing a tune called "Johnny Cope" (A general who was immortalized because he overslept and his army was consequently routed by the Scots.)

Shortly after I bunked in with the pipe band, I was informed that a duty piper and bugler would be assigned for that task on a weekly basis. Their main task was to play for Reveille and Lights Out on a daily basis, every morning at 6:30 a.m. and 11:00 p.m. The Orderly Sergeant at the Guard Room would come into our billet, awaken the duty bugler and piper of that week at 6:00 a.m. and that would give them 30 minutes to get up and be at their posts to play at precisely the right time, which was extremely important.

The duty piper that week was a fellow called Peter, and on this particular morning he had been awakened and had thirty minutes to get out to do his stuff, but unfortunately he nodded off to sleep again, and awakened again with a start when he heard the bugler play. He jumped out of bed, and as was normal, he had been sleeping absolutely nude under his mosquito net. It was dark outside so he quickly grabbed his pipes and ran 'starkers' outside where he had barely time to get his pipes up before the bugler finished his piece. Everything was going o.k.; he wasn't at his proper post, but that was fine, for the duty sergeant was seldom there. As he played his piece, he started marching along the pathway in front of our billet; marching is something that is almost automatic when playing the pipes.

What Peter did not know was that someone had been digging a ditch across our pathway the day before, and it was still open. Peter walked right into it and his rendition of "Johnny Cope" came to a screeching and wailing end when the bag of his pipes was suddenly deflated. Peter had of course both hands on his chanter and could not help himself when he pitched forward and landed on his two elbows, still holding the chanter. The mouthpiece of the blowpipe rammed into his mouth, scraping the top of it and going part way down his throat.

All of us in our beds had heard the racket outside and

got up quickly to see Peter come in. He was a sorry sight, covered with dirt and with some blood coming out the corner of his mouth. Nothing was said about this incident and another piper filled in for him for the rest of his duty. We all had a good laugh when Peter related what had happened, but it was at least a week before the poor man could play the pipes again.

There would be an inspection by Sergeant Pitkethly, and then we would be free to go to the dining hall on our own, no more being marched there. After breakfast, there would be chanter practice for the pipers, officiated by the Pipe Major. Shortly after that, the pipe band would play; we would play many tunes and practice drills and band formations. After lunch, there would be the aforementioned "quiet hour". Most of the band would lie down and sleep during this hour, but I was so full of energy from all the training I had received that I could not lie down for five minutes, so instead I would go for a run through the hills behind the camp.

I should mention that this camp was built at the base of low-lying hills that went for miles in both directions. These hills were a sacred place for the Chinese for centuries, where they buried their ancestors. The burial spots were niches carved into the side of the hill where three or four large earthenware jars were be placed. The jars, about 2ft in diameter and 4ft high, held the bones of their ancestors. Only occasionally would I see anyone visiting these sites, most probably because they were hundreds of years old. Because of the existence of these sites, there were miles of old pathways that were just great for running on.

From the pathways along the side of these hills, if I looked north along the valley in front of me towards the Chinese border, I could see on the other side of the valley some higher mountains, including a prominent peak, named the "Robins Nest". On top of this peak, an observation post had been established by the British, with constant surveillance of the other side of the border where Chinese forces were entrenched. British forces were unsure as to what the Chinese ambitions were about possibly taking over this territory by force, so we were constantly on the alert and were prepared for that eventuality.

After the quiet hour was over, the band would assemble in one of the many small meeting rooms to practice and participate in highland dancing, that was a mandatory requirement for members of the pipe band. I soon found out that several members of the band were expert at dancing, but for me it was a completely new experience, for I had never danced with a man before. This cautious feeling soon wore off as we all got into the throws of the dance. After the dance practice, we were usually free to more practicing on the chanter or the pipes.

As one can see, life in the pipe band was a bit of a breeze. The main duty of the band was to play for and entertain the soldiers in the regiment. This we would do by playing at all the parades and "retreats". The retreat is an ancient ceremony performed after a battle, when the dead were brought in from the battlefield and a lament was played for them in remembrance. This was followed by marches and sword dancing, then the band would finish off with some jigs and reels. In the olden days, the jigs and reels were to inspire the men towards greater valour in the field of battle the following day, if that was to be the case. Today it is played to honour that glorious tradition.

The regiment also had a wonderful military band that was housed right beside our quarters and they played with us, or separately during these regimental parades. This band often played some lovely music, and by listening to them often, I became a lover of military music and would never miss a chance to hear them perform.

The twelve pipers in the band were each assigned to different companies as their Company Piper and would accompany and play for them during any route marches they engaged in. Two of us would be assigned for this duty and we would take turns at playing for them as we trudged over the hills. It was easier for the two duty pipers, for all we had to carry was our pipes, while the company soldiers had to carry a lot of gear and their rifles.

It has been proven that soldiers marching behind a piper can go longer distances before tiring. If the whole regiment was going out on field manoeuvres, then the whole pipe band would lead them out of the camp and along the road to the point where they would leave the road and head into the hills to begin their exercises. On these occasions when the regiment was leaving the road, the band would countermarch and then stand and play until all the soldiers had passed. This was when all my old squadies would smile and envy me as they passed, and think what a lucky stiff I was for not having to participate in all the strenuous training in field manoeuvres. When the last soldier had passed, the band would march back to camp to enjoy a "quiet hour". At a designated time, usually late in the afternoon, we would again meet the regiment as they came back out of the hills and lead them back to camp, playing all the time.

As it can be seen, I had much to be thankful.

Unless we were on guard duty at the weekend, I would get together with some of my squadies and we would walk to Fanling and then catch the train to Kowloon. From there we would usually catch one of the Star Ferries that plied back and forth to Victoria on the island. Victoria was a wonderful old and colourful city in those days. The old double-decker electric trams still ran and the word jostling best describes the scene. Narrow streets with multitudes of banners hanging from every balcony; store fronts open to fresh air, with enthusiastic salesmen peddling their wares. Joss sticks were burning everywhere, their incense protecting their owners from evil.

I was particularly interested in watching the local craftsmen carving intricate designs and scenes on very ornate camphor wood chests. They were working right on the side of the road, doing very intricate work with ancient hand tools and doing such beautiful work. There were many clothing stores where one could get measured for a suit and it would be ready in an hour. As we were allowed to wear civvies when we left the camp on weekends, the first thing we did when we got the chance was to buy some clothes. Remembering that the National Serviceman's weekly pay amounted to approximately ten dollars, we didn't have a lot of money to work with, but we had been on the troopship for six weeks and we could not spend it there, so we did have enough to buy a shirt, a pair of slacks, shoes and socks. Besides the prices in Hong Kong were so cheap.

The topography behind Victoria is very steep; the land slopes up to a height of 1800 ft. and a funicular cable car takes you to the top. Naturally that was a "must do" thing for all the squad; and what a view we had from up there!

Most of the fellows who went into Kowloon or Victoria would go to the Army and Navy Club there. Food and drink was relatively inexpensive and it was a change from the food at camp. At weekends (the only time I was there) they had music and girls to dance with, but you had to pay them for each dance, which seemed only fair.

The pipe band had many engagements in town. We played at Government House for the Governor of the Colony and his invited guests, mostly high-ranking officers from the Army or Navy in full dress uniform. Their wives or lady friends were all beautifully dressed in long gowns.

*Two pictures of my squadies and I, on the beach ----
for the one and only time we got to go there. I look like a giant at the back,
because the fellows on either side of me were small.*

As we played for the Governor (it was usually a retreat) we could see all the guests sipping cocktails while the waiters moved among them serving appetizers; all very formal and elegant with a touch of extravaganza. When we finished performing and the applause stopped, the Governor took the salute, and we marched off playing the Regimental March Past of the Argylls', then we were ushered to the back and given sandwiches and beer.

We played many times at the docks when troopships were arriving or leaving. At one time when the Harlem Globetrotters were in town to play at the Racetrack under floodlights, the pipe band put on a half-time performance to a very enthusiastic crowd in the packed stadium. The Harlem Globetrotters did not mean a thing to me, I had never heard of them before, but to the assembled crowd they were heroes. They cheered at every move and laughed at every trick. I found out that the Chinese are very fond of basketball and that it was played competitively in every school in Hong Kong. In a place where flat land is at a premium, the advantages of basketball are obvious; it could be played indoors or out, and the cost of equipment was minimal.

For that evening's performance, a raised basketball court had been constructed in the stadium, so everyone had a great view of the game. It was the first time that I had been in such a large crowd of the locals, and I was impressed by their politeness, cleanliness and neatness of dress.

In 1951 the city of Victoria, although Chinese, had a distinctly cosmopolitan flavour. Kowloon on the other hand was less cosmopolitan, and when leaving the city by train, in only a few minutes the steam engine was puffing through the real China of old rice paddies on either side of the tracks

Peasants knee deep in the water were planting rice, dressed in traditional black suits with large brimmed straw hats on their heads. At a time when Westerners for the most part were going about bareheaded and doing a lot of sunbathing, the Chinese had learned that sun rays were harmful and caused skin cancer, so they kept themselves well covered when outdoors.

The train passed fields where the farmer would be working a team of water buffalo, preparing the paddy for the rice plants. The paddies had to be flooded when the rice was planted. Flooding was achieved mostly by gravity, but in some cases the flooding had to be helped. On one occasion I watched a small boy using a portable contraption made entirely of wood, where turning a crank handle made a series of small buckets scoop up water from a lower paddy and deposit it into the upper paddy. It was a device that had probably been in use for centuries. It was very labour intensive, but it got the job done. There was also an adaptation of this device where a bicycle was incorporated, making the pedal power more efficient and easier on the operator.

At the Army and Navy club in Kowloon, ready to take Pipe Major McGlin home after a "night on the town."

NATIONAL SERVICE: "TWO YEARS OF MY LIFE"

Life went on in the pipe band at "Dodwells Ridge" camp in the New Territories. We had to take our turn at guard duties as well as "Duty Piper". We were still classed as soldiers first and pipe band second, and in that regard differed from the members of the military band who were classed as musicians. As such, they did not do guard duty, nor did they accompany the regiment on any campaigns where danger was involved. The military band remained in Hong Kong when the regiment was deployed in Korea.

Every day "Orders" were posted on the big notice board in front of HQ, and it was imperative that every soldier read daily orders as his name may have been posted there, calling him for guard duty or some other task. He would be in for a rough time if he did not show up as ordered. Duty Piper was also posted on Orders, so we had to keep close eyes on that big board.

One day my name came up on orders with a host of other men from the battalion. It was announcing that a seven-mile cross-country run was organized to test the fitness of two hundred or so men called to participate. The battalion had taken over the grounds of the Royal Hong Kong Golf Club for the run.

On the appointed day, trucks were on hand to transport us to the Golf Club where a host of men were on hand to organize and oversee this run. We would be timed individually, and as we checked in, we would be marked off and would then start our run.

Since I had been running almost every day in the hills surrounding our camp, this run was a breeze for me. I found out next day when reading "Orders" that I was now part of a six men cross-country running team that would represent the regiment in the upcoming seven mile cross-country race held for all British units stationed in Hong Kong and the New Territories. A young officer was in charge of this team and we did a couple of practice runs before the day of the race.

On the day of the race, 100 men lined up in a large field, and when the starting gun went off, all started running to a small gate at the far end of the field. It was a bit of a sprint to see who could get to the gate first, and I managed to get ahead of most of the pack. From then on, it was basically single file running, except to pass, for the rest of the race.

This was a test of stamina; we wound through rice fields, running on the narrow dykes that separated the paddies, there was a shallow creek (two feet deep) we had to wade through, a small mountain to get over and a path through a stretch of woodland. It was tough going for everyone, even for the team of Gurkha soldiers who were running with me, and I surprised myself by coming in second in our regiment and twenty-third overall.

While running in this race, I would occasionally get a glimpse of a man at the front of the pack, well ahead of everyone else. He was dressed in white shorts and T-shirt and was setting such a fast pace that nobody was ever going to pass him. He did in fact win the race and I found out later that he was a sergeant in one of the other regiments, and he ran the whole seven miles wearing his army boots over his bare feet (no socks).

I would also find out over the course of my two years in the Army, that sergeants in the British Army were something of a breed apart from the other men; they are tough, seemingly indestructible, are also very resourceful, and set a wonderful example of how a British soldier should look and act.

The "ten weeks' training" was coming to an end, and I still did not know if I would stay with the band or join my old squad. The word came when one of my old squadies ran over to see me; he had just read orders and he said "You are out of here Ritchie, this soft touch is over, you are back with the squad again. We have all been transferred to the K.O.S.B. and we'll leave for Korea in two days time."

Cross country team.

So my holiday was at an end and I began to think that perhaps it would have been better if I had stayed with the squad and had the benefit of all the extra training they had engaged in. Perhaps I had grown soft and was not as sufficiently "toughened up" as they were; time would tell.

When the members of the pipe band heard about my transfer, they were sorry to see me go after such short time with them. There were no exclamations of "That's too bad" or "Tough luck". This was after all an infantry regiment, and it was to be expected that eventually we would be sent into harms way. They all slapped me on the back, wished me luck and hoped to see me when I came back, if they happened to be still in Hong Kong.

Meanwhile I was invited down to the NAAFI with them so they could drink to my health. Up to this point in my life I had been "sheltered" (if that is the right word) from drink. As far as I knew, my Father never had a drink of alcohol in his life. My Grandfather had taken to drink for a short while, but had long ago given it up. My Mother would occasionally have a sherry, but that was as far as she would go. Drink had never been a factor in my life, and here I was asked to go out and celebrate with a bunch of seasoned drinkers. Well, I was heading off to a war zone in two days' time, and perhaps this may be my last chance, so how could I say no.

Beer was the soldiers drink so that's what we drank. As I sipped that first beer, I thought how bitter and awful it tasted; how could anyone sit and drink this stuff all night?

It didn't take too many beers before I began to feel very light headed, and by then all the boys had toasted my health. I rose to reply to the toasts and realized that I could not stand. Fortunately I was caught by two of the lads before I fell over. I said a hasty goodbye to them all and two of the lads dragged me back to the barracks, where all I wanted to do was to climb into my bed and sleep off this drunkenness.

I told the two lads that I would be all right, and they went back to continue drinking. Even in my drunken state, the discipline instilled in me was in control and I changed into my pyjamas, neatly folded my uniform and laid it in the proper place.

All that remained for me was to climb into bed. There was just one problem: I had the top of a two-tier bunk bed, and there was a mosquito net to negotiate once I pulled myself up. This had never been a problem before, but tonight it sure was. Somehow or other I managed to get up and under the netting, lay down exhausted and closed my eyes. Immediately my head was spinning and I felt like I was falling through space. After a couple of minutes, waves of nausea started coming over me; I was going to be sick I had to get up and out – now!

I might have made it if the mosquito net had not been in the way, but I got tangled up in it and that was my undoing. I was sick from the top of the two-tier bunk, down to the concrete floor of the barrack room. This drinking was no fun at all; now I would have to get up and clean this mess before the rest of the band returned. Given my condition, this was no easy task, but I managed to get a bucket, water and mop and did a fair job of the clean up.

Yes, drinking was for the birds.

FIVE

Back with my Squadies

Two days later we were assembled in front of the HQ and again inspected. We had handed in all our gear and were once again in possession of our original equipment, dressed in our old khaki battle-dress uniforms, minus cap badges (the Argyll's) which had been handed in with the rest of our gear. We were no longer members of the Argyll and Sutherland Highlanders. Our rifles were returned to us but without ammunition, we would get that in Korea. These same rifles had been used in the Boer War (1900), the First World War and the Second World War. They were Lee Enfield 303, single bolt, with a magazine holding ten rounds, and once again we were told never to let them out of our sight. If our rifles were ever lost or stolen, we would face serious charges. For the next nine months, day or night, my rifle never left my side.

The biggest man in our squad was big Bill Thompson, and he was put in charge of our squad. If we had any complaints, he was to be our spokesman.

We were to be trucked to the dock at Kowloon, and reaching there, Military Police would meet us as an escort to a ship taking us to Korea. We were to be closely guarded; they were taking no chances that any of us would slip away to avoid going to a war zone. There was the truck waiting for us, so we loaded up and left Dodwell's Ridge as quietly as we had arrived.

NATIONAL SERVICE: "TWO YEARS OF MY LIFE"

※

Looking back at my squad, I am amazed at how little any of us knew about the war in Korea. We knew that we would join the United Nations force there to stop the aggressive North Koreans from invading and taking over South Korea. There was also the notion that we were there to stop the spread of Communism, but few of us had any idea as to what that meant, for there had never been discussion of the politics involved. None of us had seen newspapers in months, and what little we knew had come from reading the notices in front of HQ, and these notices were edited so that we would not be informed enough to ask questions about where we were being sent.

What we did know was that the North Koreans, under a militant Communist leader, had marched their army into South Korea, a separate democratic state, and had practically overrun the country when the United Nations intervened. With the combined forces of the U.S. and the Republic of Korea (R.O.K.) army, they had managed to push the North Koreans back all the way to the Chinese border, making the mistake of crossing over the border into China. Naturally, the Chinese did not take too kindly to this and they joined in the fray alongside the North Koreans, who now with a great boost to their troop strength, were able to push the UN forces back to the 38th Parallel, and that was where the UN forces had halted their advance.

This was the situation in November 1951 when our squad left Hong Kong for Korea.

The squad in the back of the truck making its way to the docks at Kowloon was oblivious to most of this. We only knew that there was fighting going on around the 38th parallel, and both sides were trying to take and hold the high ground. Many lives were lost in the taking and retaking of strategic hills. In fact, the regiment that we were on our way to join, had featured prominently in one bloody battle where a Private Speakman had just been awarded the Victoria Cross, the highest award for bravery anyone could ever get. We also knew that peace talks had been going on for several months and there was a faint hope that all could be resolved peacefully.

The truck with its cargo of sixteen national servicemen arrived at destination, the Kowloon docks, and there to meet us was a detachment of the military police.

The military police knew whom we were and where we were going; they had been through this routine many times. We unloaded our gear and they lined us up, then called out our names, counted us to ensure that no one had jumped off the truck on its way to Kowloon. That being done to their satisfaction, the corporal in charge pointed to a ship tied up at the docks, (I believe that this ship was a corvette) and said to us "We will be marching you lot to that ship over there and making sure that you board it. It's an American ship and it will take the lot of you to Korea; that is all."

They then proceeded to do exactly as he had said, and they watched closely as we climbed the gangway to board the ship with our kit bags slung over our shoulder. A group of sailors and an officer was waiting for us on board, they relieved us of our rifles for safe keeping, to be returned when leaving the ship in Korea. That being done, the officer asked us to follow him to where we would be quartered.

We followed him along the deck, through a door and down a flight of steel steps, where we stopped at what looked like a giant hatch opening. There was a railing around the hatch which was about twelve feet deep. He told us that this is where we would be sleeping, and we would access this area by going through an opening in the railing to climb down an iron ladder to the bottom. He went on to tell us to deposit our gear there and come back up to receive a pillow and some blankets.

We proceeded to do as directed, not without some difficulty manhandling our bulky kit bags down that steel ladder. One of our squadies lost his grip halfway down and fell to the bottom banging up his knee. I knew that he had hurt himself but he told us he was fine and to carry on. We would be sleeping on the steel deck of the ship, but the place was clean and warm down there. I thought at the time this was more toughening up for the squad, and this time by the Americans, but I was betting that none of the American crew would be sleeping on a steel deck tonight.

After depositing our blankets and pillows, we were given a tour of the parts of the ship that we would be using. There were the toilets, showers and wash basins, the area called the "heads" by the Yanks, and when I first saw it, I was appalled by all toilet paper lying all over the floor. I found out later that the reason for all the paper on the floor was that American sailors were so scared of catching a venereal disease from the toilet seats that everyone wrapped it with paper before sitting on it. If they tried flushing all this toilet paper down, it would clog the plumbing, so they just left the paper lying on the floor.

We were shown the recreation area where movies were being shown most of the day. There was a library and reading area, also a card room, and to cap it off, we were shown the cafeteria and dining area where we could eat at specified times. We would not go hungry on this cruise, looking at such a wonderful selection of foods that would be ours to enjoy for the next few days. Sixteen young national servicemen looked on with mouths watering, eagerly anticipating their first meal at this sumptuous banquet. With all the facilities and wonderful food on board this ship, we all had the one thought: "These American sailors are living like kings."

We were not allowed on deck, and had to stay strictly within certain areas, so our time was spent sleeping, reading, lounging, playing cards and of course eating.

Four days were spent on the ship as it slowly sailed northeast up the China coast towards Korea. On the fourth day, we were told that the ship would be docking at Inchon and we would disembark there. The weather had turned cold, so we decided to wear our greatcoats when leaving the ship.

There we were, standing on deck bundled up in greatcoats, all in khaki, wearing badgeless tam o'shanters on our heads, our big pack and small pack securely strapped on, right hand holding the rifle and the other hand holding our kit bag over one shoulder. This is what we looked like as we stepped off the ship in the rain and landed on Korean soil.

There were several American soldiers lounging around the dock area and this would be the first time that we came face to face with them. We were, as usual, "properly dressed", something that had been drummed into us since day one, and that meant boots blackened and shiny, uniform neatly pressed, wearing a collar and tie and face clean shaven. On the other hand, the American soldiers we saw wore dirty, stained uniforms, muddy boots and they looked like they hadn't shaved for several days. Most of them wore their steel helmets at a rakish angle and had a cigarette dangling from the corner of their mouths. These would be our allies in this fight and our first impressions were not too good.

An American MP (whitecap) was waiting as we came off the ship and he directed us to a truck that would take us to the railway station. This truck had a canvas cover with seats inside, an improvement to what we were used.

As the truck made its way to the railway station, I looked out the back to see if I could spot any signs of war damage. This was after all Inchon, the place where General McArthur had landed with his troops not so many months ago, and from my viewpoint at the back of the truck, I could see absolutely no war damage.

We reached the station and were told to board the train that was sitting there. Here was some war damage, bullet holes evident all along the carriages but no fire damage and all the windows were intact. This was our first indication that a war was going on in this country.

We waited on the train for well over an hour before it started on its journey, and by then it was beginning to get dark. The Whitecap came on the train with us and told us to make ourselves comfortable as we would be riding the train all night and would arrive at our destination early in the morning.

There was not much sleep for us, the train was noisy with much clanking and there were many stops along the way before we reached the Militarized Zone next morning. Once again a truck was on hand to transport us to the Rear Echelon Camp of the Commonwealth Brigade, to which the K.O.S.B. were attached, and in less than an hour we arrived at their camp. This was a large, sprawling camp of tents, large and small, and we were dropped off at the section reserved for the K.O.S.B. All men and supplies vital to our Regiment went through this lifeline. There was a lot of activity going on with supplies being loaded and unloaded, great stacks of boxes under tarps everywhere. It was winter and snow covered the hard frozen ground; in our British Army issue uniform our squad felt totally out of place. Our uniforms were insufficient for this type of weather and our hands and feet were freezing.

A sergeant major from the K.O.S.B. came to our rescue and marched us to a large marquee that was lovely and warm inside. Oh how good that felt! There we received a complete change of American issue clothing and equipment, clothing that would give us good protection from the cold.

We were given a garment that was like a crocheted vest made of string and formed into half inch squares. We were told to wear this close to the skin; it would trap the heat and keep us warm. We wore a heavy flannel undershirt over that, and then long johns. The long johns were a first for most of us; then came a heavy shirt, heavy padded trousers held up by suspenders, a wool sweater and then a long, insulated waterproof parka (with a hood) that reached to mid-thigh and could be pulled close to the body with a cord. On our feet, we wore black insulated boots with a special insole made of several layers of netting that would drain away any sweating and prevent the feet from freezing. We also received changes of underwear, heavy socks and a complete outfit of lightweight clothing.

All our "issue" packs were exchanged for more up to date ones; gone were the brightly polished brasses that we had worked so diligently on; any metal parts were now dark green, the same colour as the rest of our equipment.

The clothes and the equipment that we came with were all handed in, with the exception of hygiene and cleaning items and we were also allowed to keep some small personal items. Everything else was stored and would be returned to us upon leaving Korea, if we ever did. The only thing remaining from our original gear was our rifles. We all felt relieved and thankful to get into these new clothes, everything was warm and snug and with this new outfit, my squadies and I might just make it through the bitter cold winter ahead.

After being shown a tent where we could sleep that night and depositing our gear there, we were taken on a tour of the camp by the Sergeant Major. The first place he took us to was a large compound right in the middle of the camp. This compound was about fifty feet square, enclosed by a barb wire fence about ten feet high. Inside the compound were perhaps ten men, all probably in their late teens or early twenties but they looked much older. They were all very thin and had a haggard and frightened look about them. When we saw them, they were running around the compound holding wooden sticks above their heads. Two burly sergeants, holding long wooden batons, were in the compound beside them screaming orders and insults at these poor men. We were shocked to witness the harsh treatment that these men were being subjected, and wondered what they could possibly have done to deserve it.

The Sergeant Major answered our thoughts before we asked the question "These men" he said, pointing to them in the cage, "are the lowest form of life, they are lower than a snake, because they have committed the most dishonourable, and the most cowardly crime that any soldier could commit."

We held our breath, not daring to ask any questions. He continued "These men ran off the back of the hill when it was under attack, and in so doing they endangered the lives of the brave men who stayed to defend it. The punishment that you are witnessing will go on for several weeks, after which time they will be dishonourably discharged from the Army and sent home in disgrace. If any of you ever have the notion of running off the hill that you are there to defend, then take a good look at what will be in store for you if you do."

We all got the message and hoped we would never be put to the test. It would be easier to die a hero on that God-forsaken hill than to try to escape, be caught and have to endure the torture we were witnessing. This is exactly the frame of mind that the "high brass" wishes the lowly soldier to possess.

As we continued with our tour of the camp, the Sergeant Major would stop often and we would gather around him to listen to what "pearls of wisdom" he would offer us. He told us that we will be split up and sent to different companies in the regiment. The regiment was on the front line at this time and we will be defending the high ground that it presently occupied. We would be sleeping in dugouts at the top of the hill, and man the fighting trenches just below the brow of the hill every night, as night time was the only time when the "gooks" would attack. He told us never to allow any part of our body to be above the skyline to form a silhouette, as that could mean death. He also advised "If any of you are smokers and wish to have a puff during your watch, get down to the bottom of the trench before you strike a match."

This is where he came up with a pearl, one that stuck in my brain. He said. "Where there is light there is life, and where there is life there is death." We finished our tour with him, telling us to get a good night's sleep because it will be many months before we could enjoy that luxury again as we will be on guard duty every night for the foreseeable future. With the picture of those poor unfortunate prisoners in the cage still fresh on our minds, and all this talk of death, it was with a certain amount of apprehension when we thought about what tomorrow might bring.

After a good night's sleep, an excellent breakfast and being inspected once again to make sure that we were properly dressed, we climbed aboard a truck to begin our journey to the front line and to our positions.

※

All of us in the truck were anxious to see what the countryside in the Militarized Zone was like, so we crowded around the back of the truck to see if there were any signs of action or conflict, like a burned out truck or some shell holes, but there was none of that, just empty farm fields. The rice had been harvested and the paddies were now hard frozen.

We passed through some hay fields that still had small ricks of hay sitting there, but no shell holes. The farmers and the rest of the civilian population had been moved away from this zone, which I believe was about five miles wide. The truck went winding up some small hills and through a low pass. Pine trees were abundant up here and it was obvious that no fighting had taken place nearby.

Coming down from the hills we were now in the valley of the Imjim River; our positions were on the other side of the river on a line of low-lying hills. We crossed the river on a bridge built by the Royal Engineers, and it must have been the pride and joy of all the officers and men who built it. This bridge came straight off the high bank of the river, and from what I remember, the entire superstructure was below the roadbed. The bridge was called "Britannia Bridge". I never saw that bridge again as it was washed away in a major spring flood in 1952, but that is another story.

All the roads we travelled on were newly constructed by the Americans and were gravel roads. The road we were on followed the river on the north side of the bridge and we travelled west towards our destination, the position in the low hills.

The truck pulled into a level area at the foot of the hills where a collection of tents had been erected. The driver came to the back of the truck and called out my name: "Private Ritchie, this is where you get off."

I jumped off the truck to the hard frozen ground, my gear was handed down to me and I was told to report to the sergeant in the nearest tent. As the driver made his way back to the cab again, I bid farewell to my fellow mates as they headed off to destinations unknown......I would not see them again for eight and a half months.

BACK WITH MY SQUADIES

*A good view of the hill that would be my home,
a home with a view, for the next eight and a half months.
This picture was taken in the Summer of 1952.*

SIX

Life on a Hilltop

I watched the truck leave and waved to my squadies till it disappeared over a rise. I then strapped on my gear, picked up my rifle and tramped over to the tent that had been pointed out to me. Entering it I was met by another red faced sergeant... all the sergeants I had met so far were red faced.

In his case, the reason for the red face was obvious, he had a glowing red heater going full blast in the tent and it was very nice to step in there and feel that heat. I put my gear down, stood to attention in front of the table he was sitting at.

"Private Ritchie reporting Sir!" I said, and handed over my paybook which contains all the personal information about a soldier. He glanced at it and said:"You have been assigned to Support Company Private Ritchie, and as the name implies, we are here to give support to any part of the regiment out there who needs and requests our help. At this time, we are charged with defending Headquarter Company and that will be your task. You will be joining the Pipe Band Section that is dug in at the top of the hill. At the moment, the Section is not in their positions; they are working on some barb wire defences at our second line of defence and will be back some time later on. I want you to go up there and dig a hole in the ground where you can defend yourself, and also a place where you can sleep, when and if you get the chance."

When I enquired about a pick and shovel with which to dig this hole, I was met with a blank stare, and then he said "Use your initiative and learn to scrounge." He led me out of that deliciously warm tent into the bitter cold frosty outdoors, pointed to a path and said. "Follow that path to the top of the hill and you will come to a small valley close to the top; that is where the Section is dug in.... now go dig."

I started up the path thinking how lucky I was to have been assigned to the Pipe Band once again, but began to have second thoughts when I recalled these stories I have read of the lone piper leading the troops into battle, the sound of the pipes leading them on to great feats of valour. In the days of swordplay, this scene seemed quite admirable, but in today's type of warfare, it was totally absurd . The first person to be shot would be the one making all the noise, the piper.

These were the random thoughts that went through my head as I climbed the steep path. No trouble keeping warm, for with all this insulated clothing that I was wearing and the gear I was carrying, I was close to bringing on a sweat.

At the top there was the little valley, and there were the dugouts of my section compadres. The ground was covered in snow, a very dry powder drifting around. Some of the dugout mounds were completely covered in snow and looked more like igloos.

Now for the task at hand, how to dig myself a dugout in the hard frozen ground without a pick or spade. Scrounge he had said, so I ranged all over in my search, but the only thing I could find was a short steel barb wire picket, a tool completely useless for my task. I was rescued from my dilemma on how I was going to dig myself a bunker, and how I was ever going to defend myself if the enemy suddenly came at me from over the brow of the hill. The Section, coming back from their day's labour at stringing barb wire, welcomed me into their fold.

This was to be my family for the next year, and Chalky White, a drummer in the band invited me to stay with him in his dugout. My problem of digging myself a bunker was instantly solved. Chalky's dugout was of the most rudimentary nature; it was simply a hole dug in the ground, about four feet deep, which had been covered over with long steel barb wire pickets. A tarp had been placed over them and the soil from the excavation piled on top. There was a narrow sloping curved trench leading into the dugout, curved such that if a shell landed close by, the blast from it would not go directly into the bunker. This hole in the ground was barely big enough for two bodies stretched out, and with only four feet of headroom, it was difficult to move around, but to me at that time it looked like the warmest and safest place this side of heaven.

That was the scene on the 6th of December 1951…my 21st. birthday.

※

The Section was famished after their day's labour on the second line of defence, so shortly after their arrival we all headed down the hill to eat in the dining tent. This would be my first meal with the Section and I was looking forward to it. The food was good and hot, and plenty of it, so we all tucked in. We could not tarry long in the dining tent, for we had to be back in our positions at dusk when guard duty started, so after washing our mess tins, cutlery and mug, we headed back up the hill.

Before going back, Sergeant Bradford told me to collect a couple of blankets from the QM stores, I might need them……and he was right about that; it was a long, cold night, and guard duty was a task that all of the Section participated in.

A long deep trench had been dug along the top of the ridge, and at intervals along were raised areas above the bottom, so that if you stood up in those areas, your head and shoulders were above ground and had an unobstructed view of the valley below. These areas were called fighting benches, and this is where one stood while on guard duty. If the enemy attacked, then this is where you defended your position.

Except for a brief respite when I went to Japan on R and R (rest and recuperation), I did guard duty every night for the next eight and a half months. Guard duty was usually two hours on and two hours off, from dawn till dusk, or when we were told to stand down. So it was out to that cold dark trench every night, watching and listening for signs of the enemy creeping up on us; then being relieved, making my way back and struggling into the tight confines of Chalky's dugout. We slept on top of a groundsheet that covered the bare earth. We were fully clothed and the only thing I did was loosen my bootlaces before pulling the two blankets over me and attempting to get some sleep. It took at least half an hour to warm up before sleep came, and then in what seemed in a flash, there was someone shaking me and telling me I was on.

One of the main defences we had against anyone creeping up on us at night was the barbwire entanglements strung up continuously along the front line. These entanglements consisted of apron fences and trip wire. The apron fences were erected by driving six-foot steel pickets into the ground at eight-foot intervals, and then stringing wire across as on a normal fence. Guy wires came down from the top of the pickets at approx. forty five degrees and were fastened to smaller pickets driven into the ground. Apron wires were then strung between the guy wires both at the front of the fence and the back. When finished, the apron fence was a rather formidable obstacle to get over, and we had a line of two apron fences in front of our positions. In front of the apron fence there was fifty feet of trip wire -- that is barb wire fastened to low pickets, and the wire is crisscrossed and strung tight, approx. twelve inches from the ground. In front of this trip wire there was some very fine wire attached to flares. Anyone tripping on these wires would set off a flare warning us of their presence. In front of the trip wires, mines had been planted to stop tanks from coming through.

So all in all I felt pretty safe standing in the cold darkness of my slit trench. One night, a flare did go off, part-ways down the hill from me. When they go off, they do so with a loud bang, and as I was standing in a semi-zombie state from lack of sleep, the noise and the incredibly bright light brought me instantly to alert. My heart rate and blood pressure must have doubled as I stared ahead fully expecting to see a hundred modern day Genghis Khans charging up the hill towards me with a very mean look in their eyes.

Nothing happened, the flare eventually went out and I was once again staring into the darkness. I never found out what caused that flare to go off, but I presumed that it might have been an animal.

The morning after my first "stag" (what we called guard duty) I wondered how everyone was going to wash and shave up there on the hill with everything frozen solid. Corporal Easton answered that question for me. He had rigged up a sort of stove from a jerry can, laying it flat and punching holes on the top with a pick. He would then pour in some gasoline and light it with a match.... it burned quite nicely. He had also scrounged or acquired a large square tin which he filled with snow and set it on the stove to melt, adding snow to it until we had a large tin of hot water. There was enough hot water to give each of us a large mug-full to wash and shave.

After too many nights of struggling in and out of Chalky's dugout, I decided that at the first opportunity when we had a day off, I would dig that dugout about eighteen inches deeper; it would make my life a lot easier. When that day came, Chalky headed off with one of his pals to do some beer drinking and I forgot to tell him what I was going to do.

While he was gone, I took everything out of our home and started digging deeper, carrying out the soil and dumping it on top. It took me all day to dig it all out, put the tarp back down and then move all our gear back in. The only thing that I did not have time to do was the sloping trench going into the dugout; there was an eighteen inch drop-off right at the entrance where we had a blanket hanging to keep out the cold.

It was dark when Chalky returned, and I guess he had consumed more than a couple of beers. I was flat out in a dead sleep when I heard a garbled cry and Chalky landed with a thud beside me. We had a chuckle about it the next day when he told me he thought his time had come and he was falling down a deep well into hell when he came through the blanket at the entrance.

Beer was issued to us while in Korea, but I had no stomach for the stuff and the regulars in the Section really appreciated my gift to them during their drinking sessions. We were also issued with cigarettes that came in a round tin containing fifty…. something else that I had no use for other than for betting when playing cards. We played cards a lot to pass the time, and there were moments when I had great piles of cigarettes in front of me that I didn't know what to do with, so I would bet recklessly until they all disappeared.

As I said, beer and cigarettes were free, in limited quantities of course, and stronger liquor was also available, but you had to order and pay for it through the QM Sergeant. I was told that the QM Sergeant became a very rich man by selling scotch to the American soldiers who were unable to buy this very popular liquor at their own base.

I remember quite clearly the very first time I had a strong alcoholic drink given to me. It was perhaps the coldest night of all in that winter in Korea, and it was in the wee hours of the morning when I was on stag duty, pacing up and down, stomping my feet to keep them from freezing when I heard someone approaching. The drill was that you call out the words "Halt, who goes?" and then the first of a two word password.

The password was changed every night, and that night it happened to be "Lonesome Tree" so I called out "Who goes, lonesome" and the reply came back "Tree". I responded "Approach" and corporal Easton came down the trench to meet me. He was in charge of the guard and he always made sure that the guard was at his post and that a relief guard arrived at the appointed time. I was used to him coming, but not in the middle of my watch. When an NCO addresses you, he never calls you by your first name, it is usually "Private" or in my case sometimes "Piper". He said "The coldest night yet Piper, and I've brought you something."

He was carrying an earthenware jug and a small glass and he proceeded to pour a generous measure and said "Drink this."

I had no idea what was in the glass, but when a corporal orders you to do something, you just automatically do it. So I took the glass and downed whatever was in it with one huge gulp. He had given me a large measure of 100 proof Navy Rum. So when I hear the phrase "fire in the belly," I know exactly what the person is talking about; I have been there. For the rest of my watch, the cold feet were forgotten and my sinuses had never been clearer.

The pipe band continued to function. Many mornings

after breakfast we would go into that lovely heated tent and do chanter practice. That is where I first met Pipe Major Dougal McKinnon, a man of medium build and weight, with dark wavy hair, and I guessed his age to be between 35 and 40. His face had a perpetually sad look, with dark circles under his eyes and when he spoke his eyes would bulge out.

Because of that we nicknamed him Dugsbaws (dog's balls) behind his back, but for the most part he was referred to as Pipey. He walked with a spring in his step, and I was told that he was a very good Highland Dancer, a fact that was proven many months later when I saw him perform. I was also told that he had been a pilot in the RAF during the war, but had been cashiered out of that branch of the service for selling gasoline.

He was born and grew up in Stornaway on the island of Lewis in the Hebrides in the North of Scotland, and had a little Gaelic lilt to his voice. He did like to drink "the waters of life" and that probably accounted for the perpetual saturnine look on his face. As pipe major, he held the rank of Warrant Officer and as such he did not associate himself with the section on an ongoing basis. He kept company with his fellow Warrant Officers and was seldom seen around our positions. Most of the time that I spent on the hill I never knew where Pipey slept, if in fact he was actually on the hill. When it came to anything strictly related to the pipe band, then Pipey was there and in full command.

All of the band equipment and paraphernalia was stored down below in a tent, and after the chanter practice the pipes would be brought out, and we would create an incredible amount of noise as we practiced our slow marches, strathspeys and reels. When we had completed this to Pipey's satisfaction, the drummers would be told to "fall in" and we would practice as a band.

Pipey told us one morning that in a few days time the

band would be "on Parade" for the field investiture of the Victoria Cross to Private Speakman of the K.O.S.B. He had just been awarded this greatest of all medals for bravery for the single handed charging and attacking the enemy when the hill he was defending with his company was about to be overrun. His actions had resulted in the enemy attack being repulsed.

Private Speakman was wounded several times during this action and was recovering in a hospital in Japan. He was coming back to join his regiment briefly before being flown to London where the Queen would officially pin on his medal.

That day came shortly afterwards and it was a bitter cold day, impossible to play the pipes wearing our thick, heavy padded parkas, so Pipey decided that we should pay proper respects to Private Speakman by being properly dressed. To his way of thinking, that meant wearing our kilts and khaki shirts with sleeves rolled up. It would be impossible for us to stand out in the bitter cold and play dressed like that. So it was arranged that we would stay in the heated tent until the last possible moment and then go out quickly and play the Regimental March Past and General Salute.

This we managed to accomplish, but only just, half way through the piece I lost all feeling in my fingers and it felt like I was playing with no fingers; it was indeed the strangest of feelings.

※

Christmas and New Year (1952) came and went, and the only thing that made it different from the other days was that we were served Christmas duff smothered with custard, and we were given gloves, scarves and balaclava helmet-liners knitted for us by women in Britain.

LIFE ON A HILLTOP

A month after I arrived at the section, a new man reported for duty. His arrival coincided with our section now being moved along the hill to new positions that had just been vacated by another section. By this time I was getting tired of Chalky White's drunken habits, and as I was feeling sorry for this new man who had just arrived at the front, a National Serviceman like myself, I suggested to him that we select one of the new dugouts and move in together. He greatly appreciated my asking him, and this is how I met Dan Brown, who was to be my 'mucker' (buddy) for the rest of the year. Dan came from the town of Galashiels in the Border District of Scotland, and he was a carpenter like me. He had been assigned to the band because he was able to play the tenor drum.

The dugout that Dan and I found was much superior to the one I had with Chalky. It had been dug into the side of the hill and had five feet of headroom, it also had an opening which was called a second line of escape if our front entrance got blocked by enemy action, and this opening looked down to the marquee at the bottom of the hill.

The roof was built of stout logs over which three feet of dirt had been piled. I immediately improved the entrance by building some dry stone retaining walls. I also rigged up a small built-in table by the window opening and a couple of empty ammunition crates served as chairs. A two-tier bunk had been built-in against the back wall; it was made of steel pickets, with signal wire woven back and forth to form a nice web on which to lie. This new dugout was like a palace, and we called it "The Palace".

To greatly add to our comfort, there was even a heater rigged up to keep the place warm. This heater was a rather simple but ingenious device that worked surprisingly well. Made of an empty gasoline can that had some holes punched, it stood upright in a niche in the wall. Into the top of this can a short length of ¼ inch copper pipe had been inserted, then a length of thin rubber tubing was slipped on to the end of the copper pipe. This rubber tubing was led outside and up on to the top of our dugout where it was inserted into a can of gasoline. The gasoline ran down the pipe and was constricted by a piece of bent wire so that only drops of gasoline could fall into the can below where it was lit.

It was quite a dangerous setup, but it worked just fine for Dan and I during the cold winter months. I should mention that a chimney was attached to that heater, going up through the roof of the dugout; without that chimney, the fumes would likely have killed us.

To this day, I still have the greatest respect for the person who made that simple heater, and often wonder how he managed to scrounge the necessary parts (the copper pipe and rubber tubing) to make it work.

※

Along the ridge, a Centurion tank was dug in with only its turret and gun peeping over the top of the ridge. Every afternoon this tank would fire off a dozen or so shells at real or imaginary targets over the other side of the valley, and consequently on most afternoons a couple or so enemy shells would sail over our positions trying to take out this tank. Fortunately for us, the targeting of the enemy guns was not very good and most of the shells were wide or short, but occasionally one would come too close for comfort, and the closest one actually blew our chimney away.

Every day we would see Allied planes flying over the enemy positions on the other side of the valley; they were spotter planes taking pictures and relaying important information back to their base. These spotter planes were mostly of the American Harvard class. The actual bombing of enemy entrenchments was carried out on a regular basis by American and Australian fighter bombers. They were both quite different in the way they attacked the enemy positions; the Americans would stay up at a high altitude, above the range of the enemy anti-aircraft guns when dropping their explosive and napalm bombs. The Australians would swoop down close to ground level to deliver their bombs, which was a much more daring and exciting way to carry out their task.

The Chinese and North Korean Army employed labour battalions to re-dig their positions after a bombing raid. This was done at night under cover of darkness, and from my lonely position on the hill I could hear the occasional clink of a pick hitting rock as I stood at my silent vigil.

The only real attack that came to try retaking the high ground that we held came in March 1952. The days had been clear with above zero temperatures and most of the snow had gone, but the nights remained cold.

I was fast asleep when Corporal Easton came to our dugout and yelled. "Everybody stand to." which meant get out to your fighting bench pronto and take your Bren gun, a case of ammunition and hand grenades, both fragment and phosphorus. This was the real thing, the enemy was attacking; when I got to my position (had to make two trips) and looked out into the valley below me, everything was lit up by the many flares fired.

I should explain how our regiment was deployed along the front that we were defending. I was with Support Company that was dug-in along the ridge on the high ground. In front of us on the slope going down into the valley were Companies A,B,C, and D dug in on knolls that rose up close to the bottom of the slope. These knolls were completely surrounded by barb-wire and other defences, but were by no means impenetrable because the Chinese had great superiority in manpower.

I could hear and see the gunfire, mortar and grenade fire, and adding to this racket, the field guns behind our lines had started shelling the enemy positions. They had all the co-ordinates and positions of the enemy on their maps.... lucky for us. There was a lot of dust and debris in the air, so that after a while it was difficult to see what was going on out there.

That was when the adrenalin started to flow freely, not knowing whether the positions had held or if the enemy had broken through and were now coming at us on top of the hill. It was white-knuckle time for me as I stood there with a Bren gun in my hands with very limited ammunition. The section had been assigned three Korean porters who brought water and supplies up the hill on a daily basis; they were supposed to bring us ammunition at a time such as this, but at the first sign of an attack all three of them took off and were nowhere to be found.

Fortunately the forward positions held, and the attack failed, but we did not know that at the time, we continued to "stand to" all night, listening to the noise of gunfire; waiting and fearful of seeing the enemy coming into view below our positions.

Eventually the gunfire stopped but flares still lit up the valley below and there was still a lot of dust in the air. We stood at our posts till dawn when we were given the all clear and ordered to "stand down" and get some sleep. Apart from the occasional shell coming our way, this little episode was as bad as it ever got for me. It was guard duty every night, two hours on and two hours off from dusk until dawn. The Peace Talks were still going on at Panmunjom - they were on again off again for many more months till an agreement was finally signed.

It was early February but still bitterly cold, the ground hard frozen, when a team of doctors arrived at our positions.

Attached to the Commonwealth Brigade and traveling along the front line, testing some of the soldiers in each of the regiments who had been there all winter, they wanted to assess how fit these regiments were and how they stacked up against one another. Six men from each company would be tested, and it so happened that Dan (my mucker) and I were chosen to represent Support Company.

In due course, Dan and I made our way down the hill to the large marquee that had been set up on our parade ground. The doctors were all there with their equipment ready to start the testing, and it was a simple enough test.

Two steps led up to a wood platform. A man wearing a backpack containing fifty pounds of sand was wired up to record blood pressure, heart rate etc. and would start stepping up to the platform and then back down again, up and down for a specific length of time, or until his legs could go no further. This was explained to Dan and I as we were stripping down to our long johns to do this test. Dan had acquired a pair of long flannel underpants that he wore over his long johns - they told him he could keep them on. We then put on our backpacks, were wired up, and in our stocking feet we started moving when the officer in charge shouted "Commence test".

There were two of these step platforms, so Dan and I were stepping side by side with our hands holding the handrails on either side as we were directed to do. I noticed Dan's flannel underpants starting to slip down; the elastic must have been weak or something. Dan felt them go too, but could do nothing about it for his hands were firmly clasped on the handrails and were to be kept there as instructed.

He looked at the Sergeant Major who was also overseeing this test; he glared at Dan and said "Don't even think of stopping soldier, this is a test, so complete it. The flannel underpants slipped down to Dan's ankles and he struggled on, not being able to step out of them. I was inwardly in a knot, as I tried not to look at Dan. The Sergeant Major standing directly in front of us could see no humour in this situation at all, so I had to keep a straight face or he would be on my case, something that had to be avoided. It wasn't until we were dressed and out of that tent that we could let it out. The humour of that scene kept us laughing for days afterwards.

It was now the beginning of March. I had been in these positions for three months, and the rest of the section even longer. We had worn the same clothes all during that time, day and night. So when it was announced that there was a shower unit two miles away, we were overjoyed and anxious to get there as soon as possible. It was also announced that we would get a complete fresh set of clothing at the same time.

It was a two hour trip allowing one hour each way, and no more than two men could travel together. Every hour on the hour two men would leave, so that at no time there would be more than four men absent from our positions.

When we set off, we carried our rifle as always along with some extra ammunition, some food in the form of American K rations and some light weight clothing - all carried in a light weight back pack. Dan and I set off at the appointed time; the route was cross country to a low valley set between low hills and we would eventually reach the shower unit if we stayed on that course. This whole area was farmland with terraced paddies and some open grazing fields. The crops had all been harvested for stubble was all that could be seen.

Close to the valley we came to a farmhouse built of stone

and plastered over; the roof was thatch, not unlike the old highland thatched cottages in Scotland. There was one major difference, it was a two-storey house with the bottom storey partly dug into the ground, and animals had obviously been housed in this lower part. Right in the centre of the house there was a low tunnel about four and a half feet high. I was curious and went into this tunnel to find a high fireplace in the middle of the tunnel with the chimney going out the back of the house. On top of the tunnel above the fireplace was a large slab of slate about four feet square; this was also the floor of the dwelling above.

I was curious about all this and decided that it was some sort of heating system; a fire would be lit below which heated the slate above it, which in turn heated the house above it. The farmhouse was completely empty, the owners had taken everything with them (and I didn't blame them) when they had been forcibly moved from the Militarized Zone.

Outside the farmhouse were some ancient farming implements that looked like they belonged to the stone age, and there were also some very large fireclay pots sitting here and there that had probably been too heavy, or bulky, to move. It was interesting looking at that old farmhouse and trying to visualize what life would have been for these people before this war came along, but we had to get going and stop dithering along the way, we were being timed.

Shortly afterwards we reached the shower unit. It was a collection of tents with boardwalks running between them. After checking in, we were told to take off all our clothes and hand them over. We were handed a towel and told to follow the boardwalk to the showers, soap and washcloths would be there; shower up, get dried off and come back in for a new set of clothing. It must be remembered that it was still very wintery, the ground we had walked over to get here was frozen solid, and we would have to go outside in the buff and very quickly run over the frozen boardwalk to get to the showers.

That shouldn't be a problem for the showers will be lovely and warm, we can luxuriate under them for a while and get nicely warmed up again, so we thought. Wrong !.....When we reached the showers, our bodies cooling rapidly on the way, we threw our towels on a bench and stepped under one of a row of jury rigged shower heads set up in the tent. When we pulled the rope to start the hot water flowing, instead of shower coming out, it was as if someone was pouring water from a small teapot and it was boiling hot; we could forget about standing under that. We washed ourselves down using the soap and washcloths that were there, but we did not dally long, it was freezing and this was no fun at all. We made a mad scamper back to that heated tent and it was with the greatest of pleasure that we changed into fresh clean clothes.

With March came warmer weather, the snow and frost disappeared, the ground warmed up and the nights got shorter. Instead of two hours on and two hours off for guard duty, it was changed to four hours on and four hours off. This change was indeed a luxury for us, four whole hours of sleep was a trip into heaven.

The greening of our barren hill and the countryside around begun. About mid-March the rains started. Up until then the only precipitation we had was in the form of snow, and following the last snowfall, there had been a long dry period of cold and clear weather. When the gentle rains started, it was a clear signal that the long, cold winter was over.

※

We were issued with some new clothing, heavy cotton trousers and tunic top with a belt; the colour was somewhere between grey and light green. As the nights got warmer, we gradually dispensed with the heavy padded parkas and trousers and finally handed them in.

We were also issued a heavy poncho and a wide brimmed hat to protect us against the increasingly heavy rain showers. It was perhaps not what one would call a monsoon but it came close. The rains came steady, sometimes lasting for days. Our once formidable and solid dugout, our home, started to show signs of collapsing. The three feet of soil piled on the roof became saturated and the main beam through the middle of our roof started to sag. Fortunately no water came through to add to some of the other miseries that we were having, because the previous builders had put a groundsheet over the logs before piling on the dirt. Dan and I were quick to get a support post under that beam before it broke from all the extra weight that was put on it. It was not without some anxiety that we slept under that roof at night while the rains poured steadily outside.

With the warmer weather melting the snow in the mountains east of us, and the steady rains, the Imjim River, just a short way from the bottom of our hill, rose in a dramatic fashion. There was no flood control on the Imjim, so it simply rose up and flooded all the low lying land along its path, including all the land below us from the bottom of our hill to the river, as well as the road that I had travelled to get to these positions. We became firmly marooned on our hill with the water coming to within twenty feet of our tents at the foot of our hill.

That wonderful bridge that the Royal Engineers had built, the Britannia Bridge, was swept away in the flood and we were now cut off from everybody. At that point, if the Chinese had decided to attack, we would certainly have been at their mercy and would quickly have been overrun. Looking back, I am sure that the Chinese had their own set of problems to deal with on their side of the valley.

NATIONAL SERVICE: "TWO YEARS OF MY LIFE"

✳

When the flood was at its height, we went down to the foot of our hill to check out the situation and also to eat; we never did want for food. The floodwaters had risen up and formed a new beach just below the main tent, and lots of flotsam was eddying onto this little beach. This flotsam consisted mainly of small haystacks and matted straw, and as we watched, we could see that it was literally crawling with life; the little beach was covered, and I mean covered so that you could not see the ground. There were bugs of every imaginable shape and colour, there were snakes of all kinds, big and small. There were mice and rats by the dozens coming ashore from this flotsam as soon as it touched land. Every living thing that could crawl or run and had landed on our little beach was trying desperately to get off this barren beach......which was in fact our roadway and parade ground. They were fleeing to the relative safety of grassy clumps a little ways off. These creatures that were mortal enemies in the natural world had lived in peace on the flotsam, the hunting of prey forgotten as they concentrated on one thing only -- that of survival. Perhaps we humans could learn something from them.

During this wet period, we were left pretty well on our own (apart from our guard duties). American K rations were brought up to us by the porters, and there was beer and cigarettes for those who indulged. We spent most of the time playing cards or engaged in idle chatter; life as a soldier includes long periods of idleness and boredom. Signing up as a regular soldier after my stint as a National Serviceman was certainly not in my future plans. It is certainly not a good idea to keep a soldier idle for too long, as morale begins to drop and the soldier gets apathetic.

The "High Brass" knows this only too well and as soon

as the river dropped and our supply lines were restored by means of a Bailey Bridge over the Imjim, the section was organized as a work party to build a second line of defence, and there was also plans for yet a third line of defence. The thought of moving off this hill and going somewhere other than the bottom of it to eat or for band practice was an intriguing and exciting thought for me. Digging with a pick and shovel was something that gave me a great deal of pleasure. It was very good physical exercise, and in digging a trench there was a certain amount of pride and a sense of accomplishment in creating a trench that had smooth vertical sides. My Dad was a grocer, but he received a great deal of pleasure from gardening and getting his hands in the dirt. I was no different, and was looking forward to starting this work, while the rest of the section was grumbling around me.

From our position at the top of the hill, if we looked west on a clear day we could see the barrage balloons that flew over the large tent at Panmunjom where the on again off again "Peace Talks" were going on. These talks had been going on for months now and we were all happy to know that both sides were still talking. If they could reach an agreement, then that would be our best hope of getting out of Korea alive. What we didn't know was that it would be more than a year before that final agreement was reached on July 27, 1953.

The American military published a small weekly newspaper that kept their soldiers up to date as to what was happening back in the USA. Most of the content in this paper was about how the Yankees, the Dodgers and all the other sporting teams were performing, then on the back page, a small reference to the progress of the war going on in Korea with the usual headlines "No Progress at Panmunjom". A copy of this newspaper the "Stars and

Stripes" usually found it's way to our positions when it was about ten days old.

It seems almost a tradition in the Army to keep front line troops, especially the lower ranks, completely oblivious of where the positions they are expected to defend are located on a map. Never once in the ten months I was there, was a map of any description shown to me. Nor did anyone ever show me a map showing where this second line of defence we were digging was located. God help me if I ever had to make my way back there on my own; I didn't have a clue.

The normal procedure on the days that we went to work on this second line of defence was that after breakfast, we would load up a truck with barb wire, steel pickets, picks and shovels, American K rations, water and anything else that we might need. Then everyone under the rank of corporal would pile into another truck and head off to destinations unknown. Unless one was sitting at the back of the covered truck taking careful note of where the truck was heading, it was impossible to know where the truck actually finished up. No doubt, it was our youth and fatalistic attitude that we all held, that not being aware of all these details seemed unimportant.

Once the truck arrived at its destination, everyone jumped out and Corporal Easton showed us where to dig the trenches and lay the barb wire. Corporal Easton was an old soldier, not old in age but old in experience; he had been on many campaigns with this regiment, so he was the one we turned to for advice whether it was digging or erecting apron fences or trip-wire. The soil on that hill was lovely red in colour, practically no rocks; it was a pleasure to dig stripped to the waist, working up a good sweat. When ordered to break for lunch, we were more than ready to tuck into those American K rations which came in cardboard boxes, with food in six small cans inside. The

LIFE ON A HILLTOP

variety would vary from box to box, and we would swap cans with one another according to our tastes. These cans contained meals like "Ham and Lima Beans", "Frankfurter and Red Beans", "Chicken and Noodles", "Beef Stew", "Fruit Cocktail", "Peaches", etc. and there were always a couple of cans of soda crackers. Included in the pack would be toilet tissue, a small can opener, matches, salt, pepper and ketchup. Some of the squad complained about this food, but I always found it quite tasty and so American, quite different from the British food that we were given back at our regular positions.

This hill where we were digging had been held by the Chinese or North Koreans at one time, and their dugouts or foxholes were still there. They were quite different from the ones that we dug and were much superior if one had to cope with bombing and heavy shelling.

To give an example of their construction, they would dig straight down like a well, about two and a half feet in diameter and when they reached a depth of about seven feet, they would tunnel at right angles for a few feet and then carve out a chamber about six feet square and perhaps four feet high. I did go down into one of these foxholes, not without some apprehension, not knowing what I might find down there.

There was no smell coming out of that hole, which meant that there were no dead bodies down there, and besides, the Chinese were not known for setting booby traps as the Japanese had done during the last war. There were footholds and handholds, so I lowered myself down into that hole, full of youthful curiosity.

When I reached the chamber down below, I found it completely swept clean except for a bandolier of rice that had somehow been forgotten. It was common knowledge that the Chinese could live for days on end on a steady diet of nothing but rice while staying down in these deep holes.

It was surprisingly cozy down there in the red earth. The light coming down the well of the opening seemed to magnify as it hit bottom and spilled over to give the chamber a surprising amount of light. As I sat there, I remember thinking that realistically we could not beat these men if they had the armaments and backup that we had at our disposal. Their dedication, discipline and survivor skills were far superior to ours. These random thoughts and thinking of the somewhat precarious position I was in, rekindled my desire that the Peace Talks at Panmunjom would soon bear fruit.

My two companions on that "hill of the red earth" were my mucker Dan Brown, whom I have mentioned before, and a young soldier of twenty one named John Reid.

John was a regular soldier; he had known no other life but the army. His father was a regular soldier before him and had been killed in Europe during the Second World War. His mother had sent John to the Victoria School of Piping for boys, and after several years there he had lost contact with her. When he came of age, he joined the regular army as a piper in the K.O.S.B., and when I met him, he held the rank of Corporal. Although young, John had a fondness for drink, that inevitably got him into trouble and he was put on charge for being drunk and disorderly. He was reduced to the ranks from Pipe Sergeant but since then, he had been elevated back to his present rank of corporal. Like most soldiers, John had a fatalistic and cavalier view of life, which I thought unfortunate, for he possessed such good humour and charm. With all his years of piping John was indeed a first class piper, and as I found out later a remarkable and outstanding Highland Dancer. I watched him perform many times; his favourite dance was the "Ghillie Callum" which he performed with such lightness and grace that it was a delight to watch him. John was a handsome man by all standards, six feet tall with a strong but lithe build. He had blondish wavy hair and bright blue eyes his skin was fair and clear and he had the high cheekbones of some Nordic ancestor.

These were my two companions on that hill of the red earth as we dug our second line of defense, a line that we hoped never to occupy.

When the slit trenches were finished to the satisfaction of Corporal Easton, the good corporal then marked out where our sleeping quarters were to be dug. The only advice coming from him regarding their construction was "make them deep" so we decided to build a three men impregnable bunker. We thought at first of building in "Chinese fashion", but upon careful consideration of this design, we could not quite figure out how it would be possible to dig a two and a half foot diameter well down to a depth of seven feet, and the work of getting all the soil out of the horizontal part

So we decided instead to dig a deep trench which would be seven feet long, five feet wide and seven feet deep. All the spoils from the digging would be placed over steel pickets on top of the dugout. We would enter the dugout by means of a long sloping trench with steps at the end. Along one side of the dugout would be a three tier bunk using steel pickets and signal wire.

We worked long and hard on this project and when finished it, we even had a name for it: we called it "The Grave".

In one of my letters to Mother I wrote her about this dugout and what we named it. She was not at all pleased with the name we had chosen and told me to change it right away.

We did get a chance to sleep in this dugout for two nights when half the section was sent out to finish the barb wire defenses. John, Dan and I drew lots as to which of the three bunks we would sleep in. I drew the middle bunk and I thought that I had picked a winner.

Dan, John and Jim at out 2nd. line of Defense.

I slipped into my bunk to try it out and it felt quite comfortable lying on the criss-crossed signal wire. However, the real test would come when all three of us were occupying our bunks. We had given the top bunk as much room as possible so that the person sleeping there would be able to sit up at a crouch and swing his legs over the side to get down. This meant that the middle bunk was rather squashed between the top and bottom bunks. John got into the bottom bunk, I got onto the middle, and Dan, who was the heaviest got into the top. As soon as Dan lowered himself into the signal wire webbing that we had created, it sagged down to within two inches of my face. It was impossible for me to turn on my side, and there was no way I could ever get out of that bunk unless Dan got out ahead of me. We had named the place well; I felt that I was lying in a coffin with the lid tightly fastened down.

This second line of defence we were working on was quite a ways back from the front line, but even so, we were required to do our usual guard duty at night. Fortunately Dan and I on guard duty together were able to stumble outside and stand under the canopy of stars for four hours waiting for the far removed enemy to come creeping up our hill to try to take over our newly built defensive positions. In that unlikely event, they would have laughed at our puny efforts at building a dugout.

Getting out of my bunk was no easy task; after Dan had heaved himself down to the ground, I had to slide sideways to the edge of the bunk, partially turn, then with a great effort heave myself out, half turn and somehow land catlike on my feet; a manoeuvre suitable for the young and agile.. Two nights in that dugout was more than enough, and my Houdini like performance in escaping from that straightjacket like bunk gave my two close companions many a laugh.

Ever since my first day in the Army when our squad was given a series of vaccinations to help our immune systems cope with the deadly diseases of the Far East, booster shots had been given regularly. When we arrived in Hong Kong, we received a new series of shots, that time for diseases that were unknown to us. Along with those new shots, we started on a daily regimen of a small pill called Palurdrine. Like many other things in the Army, the reason for taking this pill was never disclosed to us.

There was some speculation among the regular soldiers that this pill was to reduce sexual drive and to reduce every soldier to a state of celibacy. Whatever was the reason for the pill, it was assiduously administered to us. Every morning during inspection, it was handed to each man, and the NCO giving the pill would watch to make sure that it was swallowed. I now believe that Palurdrine was a new anti-malaria drug that had just been introduced, and it was successful in combating a particularly virulent form of malaria that was present in Korea.

NATIONAL SERVICE: "TWO YEARS OF MY LIFE"

I happened to be reading Michael Caine's (the movie actor) autobiography called "What's It All About", and I discovered that he had been in Korea at the same time as I, although he arrived in mid 1951. He was there to complete his National Service, like every other able bodied young man in Britain then. He arrived at the beginning of summer and he talks of going on patrol into no-man's-land on the other side of the barb wire at night, to find out what the enemy was up to. His face was blackened with a mixture of dirt and mosquito repellent but talks of being eaten alive by mosquitoes that night. The insects seemed to be feasting on that mosquito repellent and mud.

When he got back to his position and washed off the mud, his face was so swollen that nobody could recognize him. Some time after that incident, he started to lose weight and became very lethargic. Concerned about the state of his health, he reported sick and I know that in the army if a soldier reports sick, especially if he is in a front line position, he is instantly suspected of being a "skiver". That is an army word, meaning someone who is lying about a sickness in order to get relief from duty on the front line. In Michael's case, the doctors probably took their sweet time to check him out, but in the end, after much testing he was told that he had a particularly virulent form of malaria. He would be sent back to Britain for further tests and if these tests confirmed their diagnosis, he would be honourably discharged from the army, since there was nothing that could be done for him.

The tests in London confirmed the diagnosis and shortly after that, Michael found himself at home living with his parents, still losing weight and at a point where he could hardly get out of bed.

One day a letter from the government arrived at his house - they wanted him to attend a London hospital to see him and talk about his illness. When Michael arrived at the hospital he was surprised to find five of his old army buddies sitting there; they had the same illness as Michael. They were told by the doctors that at this time there was no cure for their type of malaria and that their life expectancy was 35 to 40 years. There was however a glimmer of hope: an Australian doctor had discovered that by combining certain drugs he had perhaps discovered a cure for this deadly class of malaria. He wanted to test his drugs on humans if they would be willing to act as guinea pigs. They were also told that if they agreed, they would have to sign a document holding the government harmless if they died.

Having nothing to lose they all signed the document, and shortly afterwards they were put in special beds and given several injections of these new drugs. Everyone was told that it was crucial that they lie perfectly still for the next 24 hours, and if they moved their head they would immediately get knocked out and receive two black eyes.

As Michael tells it. "I laid there feeling perfectly fine and could not resist the temptation to lift my head, which I did, nothing happened and I thought, they are having us on. So I lifted my head again and boom, I was knocked right out. When I came to, the doctor was standing there beside me holding a mirror; he held it to my face and I saw that I had two lovely black eyes. All he said was "I told you so."

When I read this in Michael Caine's autobiography I came to realize that the Palurdrine tablets that were so forcefully administered to us on a daily basis, were perhaps a means of protecting us from this lethal strain of malaria.

※

The summer of 1952 in Korea was delightful with temperatures of 70 to 80 degrees and with very little rain. Hostilities had somewhat slackened, with just the occasional shell coming our way. They were still trying to take out that Centurion tank that was dug in a little ways along the ridge from us. About twice a week there would be a bombing run over the enemy positions on the other side of the valley to keep them from getting too well entrenched.

We had a good view of all this aerial activity and could see the devastating effect it was having on the enemy positions. I could only imagine how horrific it must have been for the poor men who were occupying those positions and thanked my lucky stars that it was not us who were on the receiving end.

We did our usual band practice in the mornings, and this was a lot of fun for us; playing the pipes and marching in a band can be very exhilarating. After lunch we had the afternoons to ourselves and with the Imjim River less than half a mile away, swimming was a popular pastime.

At the place where we swam, the closest point to our hill, the river was about 150 feet wide, with a low bank on our side, and a high steep bank on the other side. The water was crystal clear and warm, the current flowed at about two miles an hour and the depth of the water was four to five feet; a more perfect swimming venue could not have been found. It was relaxing and so pleasant to lie face down in the water and just drift along with the current, gazing at the magnified view of the sandy bottom and drifting past the occasional cluster of rounded, multi-coloured stones.

Our situation in Korea was beginning to take on the aspects of a low budget holiday camp.

SEVEN

Rest and Recuperation

There was much talk in July 1952 of R and R, Rest and Recuperation leave. This leave was supposed to be granted after six months in the field, and I had been here for seven and a half months. John Reid already had an R.and R. leave prior to my joining the section, and many a story he told us about his escapades in Tokyo. The granting of this leave started to take place in the section, and all of us eagerly awaited our turn. Returning members of the section had mostly tales of drunkenness and how beautiful and accommodating the Japanese girls were.

Only four members of the section were allowed to go on leave at one time, so that our fighting strength was not diminished too much. John Reid had just acquired a beautiful brand new wrist watch; it was silver with a silver mesh strap. I was very much taken by this lovely watch and asked John how he came by it.

He said "Anyone can buy a watch here, just speak to the Quartermaster Sergeant the next time you see him in the dining tent and he will order one for you. It usually takes about ten days to get here, show him your pay-book and the cost will be deducted from there."

When I asked about the price, it was well within my reach. I had never had a good watch, one that worked and kept good time, now here was my chance to get myself a lovely silver watch, just like the one that John Reid had. And so I ordered the exact same watch from the Quarter master Sergeant and it arrived one week before my leave was granted for R.and R... what wonderful timing!

The three men leaving with me on R and R were Dan, John and Eddie Fox, one of the drummers. I could now go on leave wearing my brand new watch, a watch that looked sooooo good on my wrist. The next days seemed to pass so much slower, now that I was checking the time every five minutes.

After what seemed like an eternity, the great day arrived and we were picked up by truck just after breakfast. The truck already had ten young soldiers aboard from various other companies in the regiment, so we had to squeeze to get in beside them - nothing could have kept us out. We were in that truck for several hours as it bumped along the gravel roads. It was summer and the ride was extremely uncomfortable because the back of the truck was wide open and we were choking in dust and could see nothing of the countryside that we were traveling through. No one was complaining though, this was, after all, the normal treatment that a young soldier gets in the British army. We were going off on a holiday and the mood in the back of that truck was upbeat and happy.

Eventually we reached Seoul; we discovered where we were only when we got there, for as usual we were kept in the dark as to where the truck was taking us. The Army loves to keep its lowly soldiers uninformed and constantly guessing as to what is going on.

When we arrived in Seoul, our group looked like we had just been through a dust storm. The driver stopped the truck in the outskirts of the city and came around to the back of the truck to tell us that our plane would not be leaving for about three hours. There were groans all around, so he added that instead of waiting around at the airport, he would give us a tour of the city, especially the beach area

REST AND RECUPERATION

where there would be lots of girls. With that announcement, there were howls of delight from all of us in the back of the truck.

Sightseeing from a canvas covered truck is not the ideal way to see the sights, but eventually we did reach the beach area where we stopped at the side of the road. Once again the driver came around to the back to tell us that we could get out for a while to stretch our legs. "But stay around the truck" he shouted, "I'm responsible for you lot, and if any of you go missing I'll get my arse in a basket."

We quickly got out from the confines of that truck and created quite a cloud of dust as we shook ourselves off. It was a beautiful warm, sunny day, and there was the beach, just over a small wall in front of us. What a beautiful sight this for these young men who had spent the last 7 to 8 months of their lives defending a ridge on high ground, or been trapped on a knoll in the forward positions surrounded by barb wire entanglements. Fourteen pairs of young eyes were enraptured by this lovely scene; the beach was quite busy, we could smell the perfume and suntan lotion, and it seemed that all the people on the beach were between the ages of 18 and 22, our age, and yes, there were the beautiful girls we had heard so many stories about!

Four of them were standing in the sand about twenty yards from us, and fourteen pairs of eyes were glued to them and they smiled back and waved at us. These girls were undoubtedly the most beautiful apparitions that any of us had seen in our entire lives. For many months, all of us had been denied the pleasure of gazing at the beautiful female face and figure, and here we were, just a few hours away from the celibacy of the combat zone, looking at what we had been missing.

The girls had their black shiny hair tied back in a ponytail with brightly coloured ribbons, all of them wore the skimpiest of bikinis which showed off their beautiful shapes to the fullest. What was most provocative of all was that some of these girls were wearing nylons held up with lacy garters. For fourteen young men standing at that wall it was "love at first sight". All we could do was stand and admire, with our mouths slightly agape, as we watched these heavenly bodies cavorting on the beach or languishing on the warm sand.

We had been trained never to attract attention to ourselves when in a strange place, so there was no shouting or friendly banter, even though the girls were waving and smiling at us. It was pleasant work, standing there at the wall watching the comings and goings of all these happy people on the beach. This was their country and they had the right to be happy, but the thought did strike me that if this is their country and they are all on the beach having such a good time, why am I living in a hole in the ground at the top of a hill, in what is definitely harms way?

Later on in my life it became obvious why I was there and what it was that I was defending, but at that time my young mind was considering how unreasonable it all seemed.

Our truck driver could sense that we were becoming restless, so he called out "OK fellows, close your mouths and get back into the truck, we're going to the airport."

This driver knew Seoul like the back of his hand and he soon had us at the airport where he drove to a quiet corner away from the main hanger, to where a mid-sized plane was standing. Gathered around this plane were small groups of soldiers, whom we soon found out were attached to the Commonwealth Brigade, like us. The men were from Canada, Australia, New Zealand and South Africa. We were all going on holiday together and we would meet up with them many times over the next seven days.

In a small building by the edge of the runway we were

checked in by a Staff Sergeant who told us to wait outside with the others. We would be loading in half an hour; the plane would fly directly to Tokyo and the flight would take about two hours.

This would be my first flight, but John had flown before on a previous leave, so he was the expert. In answer to questions from Dan and I about the flight, John would tell us to watch the ground as we take off; as the ground goes by faster and faster, and just when you think it cannot go any faster, the plane will take off.

We loaded up, two seats on either side of the aisle and about twelve rows. There were no pretty flight attendants to cater to us, nor did we expect any -- for this was after all our very first flight, so we had nothing to compare it with.

The two hours went past very quickly and soon we were landing and ushered into a bus that would take us to the Leave Centre of The Commonwealth Brigade at a district in Tokyo called Ebisu. The first thing that all of us wanted to do was get a good wash and get out of these dirty and dusty clothes that we were wearing. We were not disappointed in that regard, for we were taken directly to the showers, which were breathtakingly wonderful to stand under, and where we lingered for some time.

Our old clothes were taken away and we were able to select freshly laundered jungle green uniforms. The thought did occur to me that we would be very conspicuous in the streets of Tokyo dressed like this. The only item of clothing returned to us was our boots, cleaned and polished for us. So squeaky clean, freshly shaved and our hair shiny smooth with Brylcream, we were ready to join the human race.

It had been many hours since we had last eaten, so the thought of food was now foremost on our minds as we headed eagerly to the dining hall where a sumptuous banquet awaited us. Buffet aisles laden with a variety of foods for every taste bud; salads, hot and cold entries and deserts of infinite variety. After the spartan but adequate meals given to us on the hill, this banquet was indeed a trip into heaven for us.

The rules of the Leave Centre were explained to us; basically we could come and go as we pleased as food was available all day. We were shown where to sleep; a dormitory type room with a small locker at the top of the bed. There were some miscellaneous rules about being quiet at night, causing a disturbance and being drunk and disorderly. The importance of not getting into a confrontation with the local Japanese was explained to us as well as to stay away from districts that were clearly marked with "No Entry" signs.

The Second World War had barely ended six years ago, and many Japanese were extremely unhappy about what was happening to their country. The main theme of our warnings was "Keep Out of Trouble".

By the time we got through with all the advices, it was about 9.00pm, and John Reid now took over command. He had been here before; he knew how to get around and where the places of pleasure were, so we followed him as he led us to a nightclub that was familiar to him and located close by. The fact that there were nightclubs and the accompanying dance bands, dancing and drinking was a bit of a revelation to Dan and I.

We were unaware that Japan had become so westernized, and our thoughts regarding the Japanese were something along the lines of Geisha and green tea. Upon entering the night club we were ushered to a table for six, where four beers were immediately ordered. The most popular beer at that time was called "Asahi" so that is what we had and continued to drink. My ears had picked up as we entered, I could hear the sound of a modern dance band playing the modern tunes of the day. My euphoria which was already

REST AND RECUPERATION

high, now reached new highs, for I so loved that dance band sound. Couples were dancing to that wonderful music, and that sound filled me with such tender and joyful nostalgia. I instantly realized that for many months now I had been craving these sweet sounds, and now my heart and ears were rejoicing.

Two young ladies came and sat with us; they were hostesses, and if we wished to dance, they would be honoured, Their English was surprisingly good, so we told them politely that we would love to dance with them but not with these big army boots that we were wearing. They understood and I am sure were quite relieved; they countered by telling us that they would be happy just to sit and talk with us, and if necessary get us any drinks that we may wish.

That suited us just fine, for this was to be a drinking evening for us and we kept them busy filling up our beer mugs. They told us that they were both going to university, and that this night club job was a part time one to help pay for their studies. Both of them were taking English classes as they felt that such a skill would give them greater opportunities for employment. Whoever was advising them was giving some great advice; this night club was a great place to practice their English.

John was never shy, and over the course of the evening he asked if he could sleep with either of them. I am sure that they had been asked that same question many times before, because the answer that John got was. "in that department soldier you are plum out of luck."

We were having a good time, the beer was flowing freely and I quickly realized that there was no way that I could keep up with John and Dan beer for beer, I would be under the table in no time if I attempted that. I had to find a diversion.

As it turned out that was no problem, for the music had

been calling to me all night like the Pied Piper. I felt the pull, and had to get up closer to the band, so in zombie like fashion I arose and made my way around the dance floor to where the band was playing. The beer that I had consumed was taking effect, I felt lightheaded and in a state of semi-ecstasy as I stood in front of this wonderful dance band, moving and swaying to their beat. In no time I was conducting the band, or so I thought; I do remember that event, and I also remember getting back to my table, but from that point on things began to haze over for me. Seemingly, all four of us made it back to the Leave Centre on our own two feet and managed to find our beds. I awoke the next morning fully refreshed, after enjoying the longest uninterrupted night's sleep in seven months; it was perhaps the most blissful sleep of my entire life.

After breakfast John once again took charge; he asked if we would like to go to the busiest shopping and entertainment district in Tokyo, to a place called the "Ginza". He told us that on his last trip here, he had bought some china to send to his girlfriend back in Scotland, and that it had arrived back there in perfect condition. So it was decided that this would be the perfect gift to send back home to our parents, it would come to them as a pleasant surprise, and perhaps put their minds at rest as to what their sons were up to in a foreign land.

To get to the Ginza we walked a short distance to the "Electric Train Station", which we found packed with people, and I thought at the time that we may have to wait before getting on to the train. What I did not know was that in 1952 Tokyo had the best and most efficient rapid transit system in the world. Every three minutes a train would silently swish into the station and the doors would quietly slide open, the people standing on the platform would stand aside to let passengers exit the train, and then they would board.

This whole process took no more than three minutes, the doors would silently close and the train would speed off to the next station. This was perhaps the most efficient form of transport that I had witnessed in my entire life and I was most impressed. This system was leaps and bounds better than Glasgow's buses, trams and steam trains, and it gave me some food for thought about the war that had just ended.

It was a short ride to the Ginza station and we were soon strolling along that world-renowned shopping mecca. The variety of goods displayed in the merchants' windows made me wonder who exactly won the war. Back in Britain at that time people were still on rations and living in austerity conditions, so all of this affluence was a bit of an unexpected shock to me. Most of the Japanese people we passed on the street were dressed in western style clothes, the exception being that many women still wore the traditional kimono, their hair tied up in a bun held with large combs and pins. On their feet they wore wooden sandals, the soles of which had two cross strips of wood which kept the feet about one and a half inches above the ground; very practical if the ground was wet with puddles.

We spent most of the day walking along that street doing things that tourists do, like buying postcards and such. Tokyo is famous for potteries and there were many shops on this street selling the most beautiful china, so it was a natural move for us to buy a set of dishes to send home. We watched as these dishes were packed in straw in a wooden crate that we quickly addressed and it was sent immediately on its way. These dishes would sure to bring a smile when the box was opened in Scotland.

None of us had eaten since breakfast, and as young men have pretty healthy appetites, we wanted to get back to the banquet that was always available at the Leave Centre.

However, that was going to take too long; we would have to find a nice place to eat along the Ginza.

John Reid had told us many times about the T-bone steak he had eaten the last time he was here. The rest of us had never seen, let alone eaten a T- bone steak, and from the way that John had described that steak, it was definitely something that all three of us novices were more than ready to try. We had money in our pockets and there were many fine restaurants along the Ginza, so it wasn't long before we stopped at a fine looking place with two lovely potted Bonsai trees at the entrance. In we went and were escorted to a table by a waiter wearing a tux who could speak no English. It took some time before he understood what it was that we wished to eat, but by drawing sketches and using sign language, we eventually got through to him and he smiled and nodded his head.

We took it for granted that when the steaks arrived, vegetables and a potato would accompany them, but that was not to be. It was a T-bone and only a T-bone steak on that plate. He presented us with the bill at the same time and we quickly found out that the steak sitting before us cost more than a week's pay, so we had better enjoy it for we would be ordering no more. It was a tasty steak but a bit of a disappointment as it did nothing to appease our appetite. We would have to wait till we got back to the free banquet at the Leave Centre before we could really fill up to capacity.

Once again it was getting late when we left the Centre to go out on the town, which meant going to one of the many bars and nightclubs that were scattered around the Ebisu district. It was in one of these bars that I witnessed a strange sight that was too unbelievable for me to ever forget.

We met up with a group of Aussies who were consuming bottles of beer at a prodigious rate, but to me they still only seemed to be slightly drunk. These Australian soldiers were with the Commonwealth Brigade like ourselves, and were also on leave. One of the Aussies in this group had a tiny white mouse sitting on his shoulder which he would pick up from time to time in order to dip its head into his beer to give the mouse a drink. The mouse would try to escape by running from his shoulder and getting down into his shirt where he would have great difficulty getting hold of it again. All of his mates watching these antics were doubled up with laughter as the mouse ran around the inside of his shirt. He eventually caught the mouse again, held it up to his face and kissed it.

He then held the mouse by the tail, put his head back, opened his mouth wide and held the mouse dangling by the tail over his open mouth. Whether by accident or purpose I'll never know, but the wriggling mouse slipped from his fingers and scampered down his throat. Gulping hard he said. "He's running around in my stomach, I think he needs a drink."

With that, he lifted a pint of beer and drank it down, patted his stomach and said "I think that has settled him down." This scene and happening could only have taken place when with Aussies, for they were without a doubt the most devil may care, uninhibited and fearless men that I have ever come across. We would see them many times over the course of the week, and always they would be getting up to some prank or other.

There was a fountain outside the Leave Centre with a pool around it and a statue in the middle. Just about every night the Aussies would be larking around that pool, throwing each other in and climbing up the statue. I would see them climbing up street lights and lamp posts, swinging from cross beams high above the ground, fearless in their exuberance.

The four "buddies" from the K.O.S.B. once again made

it back to their beds at the Leave Centre on their own two feet and enjoyed another uninterrupted and blissful night's sleep.

Next morning as we discussed what we might do in the day ahead, John and Dan were all for picking up from where we had left off the night before and going back to one of the many bars we were by now becoming quite familiar with. Eddie and I had different ideas, we had had enough of the beer drinking for the time being and wanted to see more of the City of Tokyo, so we parted company and I didn't see Dan or John until three days later.

Eddie and I had heard about the Imperial Palace of Tokyo from some of the other fellows in the dining room. There were no maps or guide books to help us find our way around. Presumably the Japanese fearing invasion, had destroyed all maps but Eddie and I felt quite comfortable with the Super Train, and by keeping a watchful eye out the window as the train zipped along, we managed to get off at the right stop. We eventually found ourselves by the main entrance to the Imperial Palace, but found out that the palace was locked up tight, and no visitors were allowed.

The Palace was built like a medieval castle, massive stone walls with crenellated battlements along the top. A solid stone arched entrance with a giant, impregnable wooden and metal studded door blocked further advance. This door could only be reached by crossing over a moat by means of a drawbridge. The architecture looked very familiar to me and I wondered if the Japanese had borrowed from the Normans or vice versa. By standing on the drawbridge and looking down into the moat, we could see that it was full of large beautiful carp. These golden fish (among which were some with black flecks) were milling around looking for a handout, and judging by the size of them, they had obviously been in that moat for many years.

REST AND RECUPERATION

It was a lovely day, and this area in front of the palace was busy with Japanese who undoubtedly liked coming here to visit. Along the sidewalk were a row of rickshaws neatly lined up, with their owners eagerly looking for business. I looked at the construction of these rickshaws and they were quite ingenious in their design. With the exception of their wheels, a lot of bamboo had been incorporated into their construction and because of that, the rickshaws were very light and required a minimum effort to pull. They looked just like the ones I would occasionally see in movies; some of them had small fold down canopies, and all had the two long shafts by which the owner, or his employee, would pull the rickshaw.

One of the rickshaw men seemed anxious to do some business with us; he was an older man, quite small in stature with a lean and weather-beaten body. The skin on his face was pulled tight over high cheekbones and it gave him that classic Oriental look. All he was wearing was sandals, shorts, a loose shirt and a straw hat. He kept repeating the only three words of English that he knew and that was "Round Palace Tour".

Eddie and I started bargaining with him regarding the cost, and where his tour would take us, for we were unaware of any roads going around the outside of the palace wall. With the help of some other drivers and lots of sign language we found out it was a cobblestone lane of sorts. Eddie and I figured that we would have to get a rickshaw each and the cost that he was offering was too high for us. We indicated this to him and he immediately gestured to us that we could both sit on the rickshaw together, for the seat was certainly wide enough.

At that time I probably weighed no more than 144lbs. and Eddie, who was a small man no more than 125lbs. This was going to be a two for the price of one deal. Eddie and I talked it over for a few minutes and reasoned that we might never again have a chance of riding on a man drawn rickshaw, so we quickly decided to go for it. Up we climbed and off he trotted - yes, he could handle both of us; he was small but strong and muscular.

Things were going along quite smoothly until I decided to lean back on the seat to a more comfortable position. As soon as I did that I knew that it was wrong, for the driver started to rise up in front of us, his feet no longer on the ground as he struggled between the shafts. We were going to capsize backwards in a second and he was screaming something in Japanese at us. I realized at once what was happening and immediately leaned forward, whereupon the old man came slowly back down to earth. Right away he came out from between the shafts, and told us in no uncertain terms not to ever do that again.

It was a pleasant trip along that back lane; it was quite hilly and we walked most of the way. Our driver was a happy little man and he pointed out things for us to look at as we walked along, but as we were mostly following closely beside that massive stone wall, there was not much to be seen of the Imperial Palace.

Back at our starting point we were greeted by the smiling line of rickshaw drivers who had watched us take off at the start of our little trip. Our driver must have been a popular guy, for they all laughed and joked with him as we pulled up. Our thoughts regarding never being able to ride a man drawn rickshaw again became a reality much sooner than we had expected, for it was only a few years later that Japan and most other Asian countries banned this practice, calling it a degrading and humbling form of employment. These were certainly not the words I would have used to describe these men standing at the rickshaw line; they were all lithe, strong and fit, happy and full of vitality, and obviously happy to be doing what they were doing, which was pulling the lowly rickshaw.

Over the next few days Eddie and I would make many forays into Tokyo, always by the Electric Train. With no map to guide us, we would venture further afield each day. Our task of finding our way back to the train station on the many occasions that we became lost became much easier after we learned how to ask for train station in Japanese.

On one of these forays we were walking along a narrow cobblestone street that had two and three storey buildings on either side. It was a quiet street with very little pedestrian or vehicular traffic. Coming along the street towards us was a man on crutches, and as we got closer we noticed that he had one leg. He was youngish, probably in his mid twenties and looked like he was suffering quite a bit. When he was about twenty paces from us he stopped, lifted up one of his crutches, pointed it at us and started screaming in Japanese.

Eddie and I stopped in our tracks, and as if on signal, people started to appear from nowhere and line up behind this cripple to join in with the screaming. We had no idea what the screaming was all about but assumed that this poor man had lost his leg during the last war and was harbouring a hatred towards any Allied soldier.

Eddie and I held our ground until the crowd started to move towards us, then we raised our hands in a peaceful gesture. This had no apparent effect on the crowd that kept coming towards us and now looked quite menacing. The smart thing to do was get the hell out of there, so Eddie and I took a couple of steps backward, turned and ran till we were well away from these people who seemed intent on causing some pain to our fragile bodies.

From then on Eddie and I were more circumspect in choosing where to walk; some of the Japanese people out there could be mean and that was an ever present danger to be avoided, so Eddie and I were careful to always stay with the crowds.

Two days before our leave ended John and Dan arrived back at the Leave Centre haggard, hollow eyed with the fetid breath of alcoholics. They got themselves cleaned up, had a good meal and slept most of the afternoon. During supper that evening, they recounted their adventures to Eddy and I. Theirs was a tale of drunkenness and depravity, of wine and women and possibly some song.

They were both broke and could not go out drinking again, so they would just stay at the Leave Centre till we left in two days time to go back to our positions on the hill. I felt kind of sorry for them so I said "I've still got some money, so why not come out with me and I will buy you both a drink, a sort of farewell to Tokyo drink."

I made myself a hero in their eyes when I uttered these words. John said "Great idea, lets go back to the very first place we went to on our first day here."

I said "The one with the dance band, that would be terrific." All of us quickly agreed to this idea and off we went all four of us, for Eddy was just about as broke as John and Dan, which meant that I would be buying most of the beer.

In no time, we were settled in that lovely night club once again, listening to that heavenly music, and I was in my glory, for this is how I wanted to finish my leave. But looking at John and Dan, I could see that they were restless and unable to relax, so I made the mistake of asking John if he would rather go somewhere else. He looked at me with a hang-dog look on his face and said "For the past few days and nights Dan and I have been with two of the most beautiful girls in the world, and we would much rather be with them right now, but we are broke, and seeing them again will have to remain a dream for us."

His eyes suddenly focused on my wrist, and to be exact, on my lovely brand new wrist watch. His eyes lit up and he exclaimed "Your wrist watch!"

I looked at his wrist and noticed that he was not wearing his new watch. As if to answer my unasked question, he said. "I sold my watch and got a lot of money for it."

Then with a pleading look on his face he asked "Would you consider giving Dan and I your watch so that we can fulfill our dreams? I can sell it as I did mine, and then when we get back to our positions on the hill we will buy you another watch exactly like the one you have right now. It will only be for a few days - what do you think Jim?"

I immediately baulked at the idea of giving up my beautiful brand new silver watch, thinking that if I gave my watch away now, I would probably never see a watch like that again. I reasoned with John the fact that I have only owned this beautiful watch for two weeks, I loved that watch, it was the nicest thing that I have ever owned and I didn't want to part with it but John was unmoved by my plea.

Although we were the same age, John was so much more worldly than I, and while only 21 years old, he was an "old soldier" in the true sense of the word. With his cavalier attitude towards life, John's creed was the soldier's creed: "Live life today, for tomorrow we may die."

John reasoned with me that at this point in my life Dan and himself were my two best friends, which was true, and that I would be letting both of them down if I didn't go along with his. proposal. He continued by saying "We'll go back up to the front again in two days time and who knows, hostilities may flare up again an we might all be killed or captured by the Chinese, and if that happens your watch will for sure be gone for good."

I looked at Dan who said. "You will be doing us a huge favour Jim." I thought about what John had said, and there was some truth in it; this was after all just a watch, something that could be replaced, and these two men were my pals looking for a handout. How could I refuse, so I grudgingly unstrapped my lovely watch and handed it to John and said "OK fellows, here you are, now go and have some fun"

Wasting no time they finished their beers, quickly rose and almost ran out of the nightclub.

I was never repaid for that beautiful watch.

※

Up to this point in my life, my relationships with the opposite sex had been fleeting at best. Working full time as an apprentice carpenter included working on Saturday mornings till noon. I attended night school two to three nights a week, the Boys Brigade meeting was every Friday evening, and the band practice one evening a week, where I was attempting to teach five young boys to play the bagpipe. Then there was my keen interest in woodworking in my Dad's workshop (with no power tools) where I spent a lot of time creating things from wood.

All these activities left me very little time for socializing with the opposite sex. I managed to include some fun time in my life by attending, with my pals, many of the local Saturday night dances held in my home town of Barrhead. This is where I could dance with many of the lovely girls of the town, and I would occasionally manage to date some of them for a short time. Because of the limited spare time that I had to work with, these brief relationships were doomed from the start and were always short lived.

With John and Dan gone, Eddie and I could now relax, enjoy a few more beers and be captivated by the wondrous sounds of the dance band playing all the familiar big band tunes. As the evening wore on, were able to once again make our way back to the leave Centre on our own two feet and indulge in a late evening banquet in the dining room.

About noon the next day John and Dan reappeared at the leave Centre. They were famished and had obviously not wasted any of the newly acquired watch money on food, so they spent considerable time in the fabulous dining room tucking in. We could all participate in some real R & R now as all of us were totally broke.

Instructions were given regarding our return journey back to the regiment and it seemed no time till the next morning, when we were lined up and our ID's checked to make sure that none of our group had gone AWOL. I was surprised at how many soldiers did actually go AWOL in Japan, knowing full well the harsh penalties they would receive when caught. Blending in with the native population in Japan is not something that a Westerner can easily do.

EIGHT

Leaving the D.M.Z

The plane trip and then the journey by truck to our positions seemed to happen so much quicker coming back than it did going. There was no excited talk among the young soldiers; they were all morose, deep in thought and somewhat haggard looking. I got to thinking that perhaps this so called "Rest and Recuperation" leave was misguided, the name certainly did not give reality as to what actually happened during this leave - but it did broaden my horizons.

The Pipe Band plying just below our hill, John and Pipey in front, and Jim three behind Pipey.

John, Dan and Jim ready to go on parade.

Back then to our home on the hill and to our reasons for being where we were in this remote corner of the world, far from home. Life on the hill went on as before but without the feeling of imminent danger that was present when I first arrived. We had finished the second line of defence and the high brass considered it unnecessary to build yet another line, so it was now up to the pipe major to keep us busy which in our case meant more band practice.

There was a nice level piece of ground at the bottom of the hill that was ideal for marching, so that is where we went every morning immediately after breakfast. First, a chanter practice to go over any new tunes that we had been assigned, and then out on to the ground to practice marching to the beat of the drums. This was pleasant work indeed, and a thrill that very few people ever experience -- marching and playing the pipes to the beat of a drum corps.

Afternoons were our own, and that meant a swim in the river. We had found a backwater where there was a nice deep pool with an embankment that we could dive from-- more pleasant work. Warnings were given to us constantly about the danger of catching malaria and other nasty fevers from the waters adjoining the river, but these warnings were generally ignored as we were young and felt indestructible. Besides, we had never heard of anyone along our stretch of the ridge coming down with malaria. Perhaps this was because we were constantly jabbed with needles from the traveling medical units, inoculating us against every conceivable disease known to men.

After one of these jabbing sessions my arm started to swell up and become quite painful, no doubt caused by infection from a dirty needle. Pipey took a look at my arm and told me to report to the nearest medical unit which was about two miles away. So off I went to see what the medics could do for my infected arm and as always, carrying my rifle and small pack.

Before long, I arrived at a small cluster of tents with a large red cross prominently displayed on the largest one. A young MO looked at my arm, then grunted and said "This is something I can fix."

He then swabbed my arm with alcohol, and without giving me the benefit of a local anaesthetic, he picked up a scalpel, made a three quarter inch slit in my arm right over the site of the infection and squeezed out a quantity of yellow pus. When this was done to his satisfaction, he swabbed the site clean with disinfectant, snapped a Band-Aid over the wound, grunted again and said "OK you're done."

I still have that scar on my arm.

All of our section stayed surprisingly healthy during our stay on the hill, separated from the diseases of men by our isolation. Possibly another factor that helped us to avoid all the nasty mosquito borne diseases might have been the fact that every evening at dusk, just when mosquitoes became active, we were up at the top of the hill where there was generally a breeze blowing and mosquitoes do not fly too easily in wind.

※

Life in the Pipe Band dragged on; July came and passed slowly for us; apart from daily band practices and nightly guard duties we passed the time playing cards. All our jokes had been told several times with no fresh material coming in. Our escapades during R and R in Japan had been gone into in great detail by all of us. Sergeant Bradford regaled us with an account of his visit to a high class bordello in London during his last leave there. This bordello was in a Georgian manor house in a very posh district of London, surrounded by beautiful gardens.

When Sergeant Bradford arrived there, the door was opened for him by a butler wearing a tux who spoke with a well cultivated Oxford accent - he probably doubled as a bouncer. This visit had made a huge impression on Sergeant Bradford, for he remembered every little detail of the evening spent there, saying that the cost (which would have been considerable) was the best deal that he ever had, and that he fully intended to visit there again whenever he got the chance.

Sergeant Bradford was of mixed race, half English and half Malayan; this was not uncommon with regular soldiers in the British Army, most of whom were offspring of a liaison between a British soldier and a native woman in the country occupied or controlled by Britain.

There would not be many offspring from the troops in Korea, for we were kept in tight control within the Militarized Zone at all times.

August came, and there was much uncertainty in the ranks as to when our tour of duty would end. Certainly none of us wanted to endure another bitter cold winter in these hills. Boredom was settling in with the troops, a condition that is very bad for morale - it was time to move out.

Word finally came near the beginning of August that the regiment was being relieved, and this news was greeted by all of us with great relief and pleasure. Moving troops from a front line position requires a great deal of coordination as these positions could not be left unguarded overnight - consequently, on the day of the move there was a great deal of coming and going.

Soldiers are trained to pack up and move quickly and in our case the quicker the better. It was raining on the day of the move and the tracks down from the top of the hill were slippery and muddy from what was now several days of rain. This condition did not bother us one bit - we were going home and our feet had wings.

As we made our way down the hill, we could see the fresh troops lined up at the foot of the hill, ready to take over our positions. They were lined up in three ranks - the rain bouncing off their poncho capes and dripping off their wide brimmed hats. None of them looked too thrilled at the prospect of spending time on that hill, and as I looked at them, I was reminded of a line in one of Robert Burns' poem where he said. "And forward tho I cannot see, I fear and dread."

These thoughts were perhaps in the minds of these young soldiers as they stood there in the rain. I cannot remember feeling sorry for them, I was only too happy to see them standing there ready to take over. I was exulting over the fact that I was now on my way from this place, hopefully never to return.

The trucks that had brought these fresh troops were

waiting for us, so we quickly climbed aboard with all our gear, each of us with an ear-to-ear grin lighting up our faces. As the truck pulled away from our positions, I glanced back through the rain and grey skies to take a last look at the hill that had been my home for the past eight and a half months. I looked at this hill with absolutely no regrets of leaving it.

As I have said before, the lower ranks in the Army never know where a truck might take them once they are aboard that truck and it is moving. We naturally assumed that the truck would be heading to a place beyond the Militarized Zone where we would meet up with the rest of the regiment. Instead, we headed to some other positions that were now unoccupied and these were only about five miles from the hill that we had just left.

The truck stopped and we were ordered to shoulder our gear and climb yet another hill, a distance of about half a mile and which was, thankfully not too steep. As we trudged along in the rain and mud, we passed a group of Canadian soldiers belonging to the P.P.C.L.I. who were going in the opposite direction. They looked every bit as bedraggled as we were, and like us they had no idea as to where they were going.

As we reached the abandoned positions that had been selected for us to sleep in, we discovered that these positions, (deep covered holes in the ground of the most rudimentary nature) had not been occupied for many months. We were told to find a dry dugout, and to be prepared to spend two nights in it before moving on again.

I bunked with Mike, another piper; he had found a dry dugout, but it had only four feet of headroom. I was back again to where I started, to zero in the comfort department. It was only for two nights and by now all of us could sleep under a hedge if we had to.

Guards were posted at night as usual, for we were still in the Militarized Zone and for sustenance we were given American K rations. Apart from the guard duties, we slept most of the time, fully clothed with our boots on, and in a state of semi-hibernation.

Two days later we were all back in the trucks and this time we crossed the Imjim River on the new Bailey Bridge, and left the Militarized Zone. A cheer went up in the truck when we passed out of the Zone for the last time, and I began to reflect on how lucky I had been.

Eight and a half months on the front line of a combat zone and I had not fired a single shot from my rifle -- the gods had indeed been good to me.

NINE

Britannia Camp and Pusan

As if on cue, the sun came out to match our cheery disposition, and soon we were passing through the guarded entrance of a large tented encampment. A sign above the entrance said "Britannia Camp - Commonwealth Brigade". This was the mustering point for all regiments of the Commonwealth Brigade when going into, or out of the Militarized Zone.

Our little unit from the Kings Own Scottish Borderers Regiment was one of the last to reach this camp, and we were told upon reaching it that the Regiment was being transported by rail to Pusan within the next two days. In Pusan, a Memorial/Retreat Service would be held at the Military Cemetery to honour the men of our regiment who had died on the field of battle in Korea.

Before the Armistice Agreement was signed in 1953, a total of 1078 British soldiers would die, including 204 National Servicemen.

Our band uniforms, instruments and equipment had arrived ahead of us and were now in storage. We were quickly lined up and marched there to pick up all our belongings. When this was done, our section carrying all our gear was marched between the long rows of tents and was shown the tents that had been assigned to the pipe band.

After living in a hole in the ground, these tents were the ultimate in luxury. They had wooden floors and wooden sidewalls about two feet high, and their canvas tops and canvas ends gave them a light, open and airy feeling, something that we were not used to. The interiors were spacious, holding six to eight camp cots with enough space around them for our gear.

Shortly after we had settled into our tents, Pipey came by to see us and enquire if everything was satisfactory; which of course it was. He looked at me and said:

"Ritchie, I am assigning you the task of Duty Piper for the rest of the day. You will only have to perform the one task, that of 'lights out' at 2300 hours. Make sure you are properly dressed, no need to wear the kilt but wear your pipers bonnet. Your task is to march the full length of the main pathway down the centre of the camp playing 'lights out' and you will start playing immediately after the bugler has sounded, --- that is all."

With that he turned on his heels and strode off. We did not see Pipey for the rest of the day and by the look in his eyes, he was going off to enjoy some serious drinking with his fellow warrant officers.

After Pipey left, I quickly checked my pipes to see if all was in order, and from then on I did not think much about my assignment. After all it was a simple task, one that I usually enjoyed, so I relegated this assignment to the furthest recesses of my mind.

The sun was shining, it was late morning and I was anxious to contact members of my old squad to see how they had fared during the last eight and a half months. Not knowing what companies my former "squadies" had been assigned to, I had to wander among the many rows of tents asking questions for their whereabouts.

The beer was flowing freely and I found out that it was issued free of charge so that every tent I poked my head into had a party going on in full swing. Many of these soldiers had been "in the line" for over fourteen months and many of their companions had been killed during the first four months of the regiment's tour of duty. It was a time to celebrate and drink to the memory of those companions who never made it.

Every tent I went into offered me a drink and asked to join them, so it was slow going as I tried to locate some of my former squadies. There were many men wandering about as I was, looking for friends and former friends they had not seen or heard from in fourteen months. Soldiers do not wish to be emotional in front of one another, so that when meeting a former buddy who has come through the many months of conflict unscathed, they greet each other with loud guffaws, a hand shake, a slap on the shoulder and then a drink to each others health.

I had consumed a couple of beers by the time I finally met up with some of my old squadies. We immediately went through the greeting ritual that we had been witnessing around us. It was good to see them again, familiar faces in a far off land. The three of them who were there looked much older than they did eight and a half months ago when we last had parted. Gone were the boyish looks and innocence, instead there was a manliness and a hint of weariness about them. All of them had been in the forward positions where things had been much tougher for them than for me.

When I asked about the rest of our squad, I was given the tragic news that one of us, Ian Coulter, had died. Ian had been the star soccer player in our squad and had dazzled us on many occasions with his expert dribbling and shooting. It was chilling news for me to think that one of us would not be going home and instead had finished up in a foreign grave.

Ian had contracted a virulent form of one of the many tropical diseases and had been immediately shipped to a hospital in Seoul where his condition had worsened, and within a few days he was gone. This news of Ian's death quickly sobered me up, and I said goodbye to my squadies, promising to get together with them in Hong Kong.

I then made my way to the dining tent which was unusually quiet; it seemed that the whole regiment was ensconced in their tents celebrating the completion of their tour of duty. That suited me just fine, for I wanted to be alone to think of Ian Coulter, for that vision of him on the soccer field kept haunting me.

It occurred to me that I was perhaps the only one in the whole regiment at that time who was feeling melancholy, and a little sad. I had to snap out of it, this was no time to be sad. It was time to get back and join in on the celebration that I knew would be going on in our tent, so I loaded up with as much beer as I could carry and headed back to where I knew a "bunch of the boys would be whooping it up" to quote another Scot.

Sure enough, Dan and John were well into their cups and I was welcomed back like a long lost brother with cries of "have a drink, have a drink!" So I sat down and joined in on the nonsensical conversations that soldiers engage in during these drinking sessions.

In the back of my mind I knew that I had to be careful and not get drunk, for I had that important duty to perform at the end of the day, to play "Lights Out". The R.S.M., the Duty Sergeant and a host of others would be out in force to make sure that "Lights Out" was strictly adhered to, and woe betide me if I went "three sheets to the wind" like the rest of them were doing.

To be drunk while on duty was a chargeable offence, and at this stage of the game, I wanted to avoid being put on a charge and having to endure some sort of punishment that would be coming my way if I was stupid enough to get drunk. So I played it cool and sipped my beer while all the others were sloshing it down.

As the night wore on towards the all-important 2300 hours, I noticed my mates falling asleep one by one. The ones who were left, and just hanging on, were talking a drunken gibberish to one another. Ten minutes before the appointed time I stood up to test my legs. Yes... I had managed to stay sober.

I adjusted my pipers bonnet, picked up my pipes and headed to the end of the main pathway where the bugler was standing, and where I would start my march. My pride in staying sober faltered somewhat when I got out into the fresh air and started to walk.... I definitely had a buzz on. I must have been sipping a lot more beer than I thought I did.

It was dark, and I seemed to be walking in a fairly straight line so nobody will notice me, or so I thought. The moon was out and a row of low lights defined the pathway that I had to walk along. The bugler finished his Bugle Call as I stood at the ready with the bag of my pipes filled with air. As the last note from the bugle faded, I blew heartily into the bag and gently punched it with the heel of my right hand, necessary to prevent the drones from squealing. The drones came in on cue, first the bass and then the two tenor drones; I tucked the bag under my left arm with my right hand and then got both hands on the chanter.

At this point it is necessary to squeeze a little harder on the bag with the left elbow to get the chanter come in, and it is sometimes necessary to then tune the drones to the chanter so that everything harmonizes.

Tonight that did not seem to be necessary because I could not hear the chanter sounding. I knew it was sounding because I could feel the hot air coming out of the chanter holes. I started on my long walk down through what was now a deserted camp. I had never played the pipes while inebriated, and it was the strangest feeling. The drones close to my ears were blasting out a pure sound that overwhelmed every other sound. I could not hear the chanter, and consequently could not hear the tune I was supposed to be playing. Furthermore, I seemed to have lost the feeling in my fingers; my hands were numb and seemed separated from my body.

The tune that is played for "Lights Out" is called Donald Blue, and it is a sombre and melancholy tune, almost what you might call monotonous in nature. It was the kind of tune that if you do not hear the notes being played, you are likely to go astray. I was in a pickle and I knew it, but I had to bravely soldier on and hope that nobody could hear the racket I was making….. slim chance of that unless everybody was flat out drunk.

These thoughts were racing through my head as I tried to get through this fiasco. Not much further to go thank God, but who is that standing up there at the end of the pathway? Horror of horrors, it is the R.S.M. (Regimental Sergeant Major); there he was, impeccably dressed as always, his uniform expertly pressed and wearing his red sash.

He stood facing me, slapping his cane against the side of his leg with his right hand while holding a small notebook in his left as I made my way towards him. I instantly turned to jelly at the sight of him, the most feared man in the regiment, and I could see that he had his notebook out ready to put me on a charge…..now I was in for it.

I stopped in front of him and finished what I thought was "Donald Blue", then lowered my pipes and snapped to attention. He looked at me with that stern, no nonsense look that is reserved strictly for Sergeant Majors and asked: "What is your name and number Piper" in a voice that told me, this is it Jim, you are now going to be put on a charge. What bloody bad luck that this of all men should be standing here tonight? I shouted out. "Private Ritchie 22470448 Sir.!"

After hearing me say this, he seemed satisfied and he

put his notebook in his breast pocket, buttoned it up and replied. "Ritchie, I've been in this man's army for over twenty five years, and during that time I have heard "Lights Out" being played may thousands of times, but never ever have I heard it played like you played it tonight." With that, he fixed me with that mean look of his and said. "OK Ritchie, fall out and get some sleep"

Was this true, was I actually going to get away with this? I quickly bawled out "Sir", turned to my right, brought my left foot down with a crash and quickly fled the scene; marching away as quickly as I possibly could, to put some distance between myself and this most dreaded of men before he changed his mind.

The next morning another piper who had been assigned as duty piper awakened me to the sounds of "Hey Johnny Cope", after what had been a most glorious full night's sleep. What a luxury it was, and all because I had no guard duties to perform.

※

Britannia Camp was immediately abuzz with activities. First breakfast in the dining tent, then all companies including the pipe band were lined up for inspection by the company commanders, where we were told that the soft life that we had been having for the past several months was now over. It was now time to get back into shape; there would be p.t. every morning, drilling and inspections for everyone. Most importantly, we were to get our uniforms and equipment into first class shape; punishment would be meted out to anyone who failed to come up to the high standard that the commanding officer demanded. In two days time we would be entraining for Pusan where the regiment would encamp and prepare itself for the Memorial

Service and Tattoo given to honour the brave men who had died on the "Field of Battle".

The pipe band had a major role to play in the Retreat Service of the Tattoo, so long hours were spent on drilling, practicing and perfecting the tunes that we would be playing. A considerable length of time was also spent working on our boots, uniforms and equipment to bring everything up to the high standard expected of us.

Three days later the military tradition of withdrawing to safe ground to honour the dead took place in Pusan as planned. I got my first look at our Commander-in-Chief of the 1st.Battalion K.O.S.B., Lt. Col. Tadman, who spoke eloquently to honour the 47 men of the K.O.S.B. who had died in this country, and to praise the many who were wounded in our fight to preserve freedom and democracy in the world.

The pipe band put on a good show when the eulogies ended, with our Military Tattoo drill which included "The Last Post" on the bugle and "The Flowers of the Forest" on the pipes, after which we played to the March Past of the whole battalion of 700 to 800 men.

Lt.Col.Tadman took the salute, and as I watched these men march past, I felt very proud of each and every one of them. It was indeed a poignant moment for me.

BRITANNIA CAMP AND PUSAN

This picture of the pipe band marching in the Port of Pusan is one that I like; when I look at it after all these years I can still recall that feeling of joy that all of us felt at that time, a joyous satisfaction of having done our bit and that we were now leaving Korea to go back home. Marching in the band, playing the pipes to the beat of the drums greatly heightened that happy feeling, and I am captured once again by just looking at this picture. In this picture I am in the front row, from left to right Sergeant Bradford, myself, Corporal John Reid, and Pipe Major McKinnon.

Jim ready for parade at Pusan.

The King's Own Scottish Borderers, at the Commemorative Parade, Pusan Cemetery. The pipes and bugles are played as the flag is raised. Someone took a picture of me looking for the grave of Ian Coulter at the Pusan Cemetery. I spent some time looking for his grave there, but never did find it.

TEN

Ho Tung House

The K.O.S.B. pipe band plays as the men of the regiment load onto the troopship Empire Halladale at the dockside in Pusan as they prepare to leave Korea.

Everything moved quickly from then on, and a couple of days later the Battalion was lined up at the docks in Pusan ready to embark on the H.M.S Halladale troopship. The pipe band had gone on board ahead of the rest of the battalion in order to deposit some of our gear, and then had come ashore again to play on the docks while the troops embarked. As it turned out, we were among the last to board the ship before it cast off from the dock at Pusan to begin the four-day journey to Hong Kong.

I was very much impressed at how smoothly and quickly the regiment had been moved from the Militarized Zone of Korea to the relative calm of Pusan where a ship was waiting to take them to Hong Kong. The logistics of such a move must have been incredibly complex, but this was something at which the British Army was exceptionally good.

As we sailed into Hong Kong harbour four days later, we were greeted by the military band of the K.O.S.B. at the dock, resplendent in their whites, playing our very own regimental tune, "All the Blue Bonnets are over the Border". I am sure that I was not alone in suddenly feeling a great sense of pride at the sight of them.

As I alluded to before, the military band in a Scottish regiment is very much different from a pipe band, in as much as they are classed as bandsmen and are not required to do duty as a soldier. This excludes them from entering any war zone that the regiment is called upon to enter, and that certainly included the Korean Peninsula. The military band had stayed behind in Hong Kong for the fourteen months that the regiment had served in Korea.

On the other hand, members of a pipe band are classed as soldiers first and bandsmen second, and will follow the regiment wherever it goes.

A fleet of trucks was lined up at the dock ready to transport us to our new barracks, wherever they might be, and I was thinking that we would probably be going back to Dodwell's Ridge near the village of Fanling, where I had spent ten weeks with the Argyll's before being shipped to Korea. As usual, we were kept in the dark as to where the truck was taking us until it reached its destination, which turned out to be a camp called Ho Tung House.

Situated close to Sheung Shuei, the last railway station

before crossing the border into China, it was heavily guarded by the Chinese Army on the other side. If anyone was ever stupid enough to fall asleep on the train and taken into China, he would soon find himself in a Chinese prison, and it might take many months before he was released.

Ho Tung House had originally been the home of a very rich merchant or trader; it had extensive grounds with small wooded areas and a very large area of open fields that had probably been used for cattle or horses. The British Government had somehow acquired this property and then turned it into a camp to house some of the many troops that were stationed in Hong Kong in 1951.

The British Government at the time was unsure if Mao Tse Tung and his Communist government in China were intent on taking over what they claimed was the rightful ownership of Hong Kong and the New Territories. Consequently the British Government had many thousands of its troops stationed along the border between the New Territories and mainland China to prevent this from happening.

The previous property owner's large palatial house had been taken over by Headquarter Company, and the rest of the troops, including the pipe band, were housed in large Nissen huts that were scattered throughout the property. The pipe band's quarters were located a short ways from the main entrance gates and the guardhouse.

This camp property was completely enclosed by a high perimeter fence and was strictly guarded at all times, which meant that anyone coming into or out of the camp had to first check into the Guard House. The main road, which was never very busy, ran past the front gate of the camp and it also ran close to our quarters.

I said that this main road was not very busy through the day, but we soon found out that at about 2:00 a.m. every night a fleet of large trucks would rumble along this road

HO TUNG HOUSE

and in their passing they would leave the most odious and obnoxious odours lingering about our quarters. What could possibly cause such an odour, which would wake you up at night? The answer came from a duty officer who was inspecting our billet one day, and after the inspection he asked the usual question that every inspecting officer asks: "Any complaints?"

Someone piped up and complained about the smell. The officer told us that the fleet of trucks that ran at night had just collected human waste from the hundreds of open latrines in Hong Kong and Kowloon. This waste was collected in tightly woven baskets that had wicker lids that were fastened down with straps after the baskets were filled. The filled baskets would then be stacked on trucks and transported to the fields of the New Territories where these baskets, with their odorous contents, would be carried on the shoulders of the workmen employed by the trucking company, and their contents dumped into strategically placed cesspools throughout the fields.

When I heard the officer explain all this to us, I could not think of a line of work more repulsive that these poor workers were employed to do. This "fertilizer" would not be used for some time; instead, it would ferment for a period and would occasionally be stirred before being spread on the paddies during flooding.

This practice of fertilizing with human waste, so abhorred by western society, has been carried out in China for thousands of years, and without these essential nutrients their productive rice paddies would have become barren. Now that we knew where the obnoxious smell was coming from did not make the stink any less offensive, but as time went on, we seemed to get used to it.

Life in the pipe band was now all about polishing up and improving our playing and drilling as a band. Pipey had chanter practice every morning, and I should note that over the last few months there had been several new pipers and drummers added to our ranks. Most of these newcomers were National Servicemen like me, and almost all of them had to improve their piping a great deal before the standard that Pipey insisted on could be achieved.

The only way to achieve such improvement in quality was by chanter practice, to learn all the new tunes by heart and to improve the flexibility of the fingering. This was slow going for some of the new pipers but Pipey was strict and kept them at it all day, even threatening to discharge them from the band if they didn't shape up.

For playing and practicing with the pipes, we had a quiet wooded area where we could blow away to our heart's content. The pipes are a difficult instrument to maintain; the drones are made of natural cane and the chanter reed, also made of double sided cane, makes them both finicky, especially the chanter reed. Having a good reed for your pipes was like gold, it has to be easy and not too hard to play. If the reed was too hard to play, you had to softly press the canes together and sometimes lightly sand it before getting a sound out of it.

All this tampering with the reeds and drones had to be done with the greatest of care because they were in short supply at the camp, and Pipey would get most upset if anyone damaged or destroyed any of them. The bag for the pipes was usually pigskin or sheepskin, and it was very important that it be airtight. To achieve this, it had to be seasoned with something to make it flexible; without this seasoning the moisture from our breath would initially make the skin soft and pliable but would soon dry out, become hard and start to leak.

Pipey had a supply of commercial seasoning that we used. I have no idea what it contained, but it seemed to

HO TUNG HOUSE

work for all of us. The most common ingredients for seasoning were molasses, sometimes the white of an egg, and there was always some talk going around that the best way to make the bag softer and flexible was to pour in a half of Scotch and massage it into the skin.

On weekends we were allowed to leave the camp but had to be checked out and checked in again at the guard-house before "Lights Out". Failing to do so would mean that we were AWOL and the MP's would immediately start looking for us. Woe betide when they found you, and find they would.

It was less than a mile walk to the railway station at Sheung Shuei; the railway line there continued on to Canton, China. This station was where we could catch the train to Kowloon, and when we had some time off, Kowloon and the old city of Victoria on Hong Kong Island was the place to go.

We were allowed to wear civvies when on day-leave from camp; all of us still had the civvies that we had bought on our first visit here. What did we do when we got there? Initially we would revisit all the places of interest, such as the Funicular Tram to the Peak high above Hong Kong, go strolling along the main streets of Victoria and jostle with the crowds. Once again I would like to mention that if you wanted, you could get measured for a custom made suit which would be ready for pick up in one hour; a well tailored and well fitting suit for an unbelievably low price. Eventually, after seeing all we wanted to see, we would cross again on the Star Ferry and find ourselves at the Army and Navy Club, strategically placed between the Star Ferry and the Kowloon-Canton Railway Station. This very popular venue had many attractions for young enlisted men who were trying to escape for a short time the rigours of camp life.

There was a variety of delicious and inexpensive meals that you could indulge in. Steak, eggs and chips were the all time favourite and inexpensive local beer was always flowing freely. Popular music was always being played by a very good local dance band, and there were lots of beautiful girls to dance with - you had to buy a ticket that was good for only one dance.

On one occasion, several members of the pipe band had gone down to the Army and Navy Club and were enjoying a good time. John, myself and several other members of the band had decided to wear our kilts on this occasion. As was normal dress code, none of us wore anything under our kilts, we liked the air to blow freely.

John Reid was a very good dancer, and he was up on the dance floor with a beautiful young lady, giving us a show as to how a slow foxtrot should be danced. There was a drummer with us called MacDonald, whom we called "Wee Mack". As the name implied, Mac was a very small man, and he was always up to some trick or other which would get us laughing. As John slowly glided past our table, Wee Mac quickly got up and danced closely behind John, keeping in step with every step that John made, so that John was completely unaware that Wee Mack was there.

There were a goodly number of people sitting at tables around the dance floor watching this show when Wee Mac added to the hilarity by lifting up John's kilt at the back, exposing his bare bum. Everyone was in stitches at Wee Mack's antics, and still John was unaware of what was going on behind him, wondering at what everyone was laughing. John danced half way around the dance floor before he discovered what Wee Mac was up to, and then he joined in with the rest of us in having a good laugh.

One evening at about dusk an MP vehicle pulled up at the guardhouse. As I mentioned before, our billets were close to the guard-house so those of us who were standing around at that time had a good view of what went on around this entrance gate. Two MP's, smartly dressed as always, went to the rear of their vehicle, opened up the double doors and let out a handcuffed prisoner. The prisoner was wearing a kilt, in fact he looked like he was wearing full highland dress but this was difficult to make out since the man was covered in filth or mud from head to toe. He looked like he had fallen into a paddy.

Whatever he had fallen into stank to high heaven, for we could smell him from our distance, but whoever he was looked vaguely familiar. It wasn't till next morning after breakfast when chanter practice was about to begin, that instead of Pipey overlooking the practice, it was Sergeant Bradford who went on to tell us that Pipey would be indisposed for a day or so due to a misfortune.

We found out the whole story later on; it was Pipey who had arrived at the guardhouse in handcuffs.

The story went like this: Pipey had heard from one of his fellow warrant officers that there was a lovely lady who lived in a nice house about a mile from Ho Tung House, and she was giving favours to some of the other warrant officers in the regiment. Pipey's ears had pricked up at this juicy piece of information, so he decided to go out and try his luck. He wanted to look his finest in this quest, and decided that full highland dress was the answer ... to his way of thinking no woman could resist a man dressed like that.

He had learned that the house where the lady lived was at the edge of a series of terraced paddies, which at that time of the year were dry. He was told that he just had to go to her home, and if she liked his look, she would invite him into her house, and best of all, the price she charged was most reasonable.

So off went Pipey in full highland dress to have a secret liaison with this beautiful lady. What Pipey did not know was that the Military Police had heard about this house, posted the area off limits, and were keeping it under surveillance.

It was not known whether Pipey was going to or coming from the house when he was spotted by the MPs, who always enjoyed spoiling a man's fun. They gave chase, and as they were some distance off, Pipey figured that he could outrun them and perhaps escape from their clutches. He was usually very nimble on his feet, but I suspect that Pipey, who was very fond of whiskey, had just recently consumed several glasses of "The Waters of Life" and was quite drunk and slower to move.

The story goes on that Pipey was running along a narrow earthen dyke that separated two of the paddies and when he reached the intersection of yet another paddy where a cesspool full of human waste was located, he somehow lost his balance and fell headfirst into this odious cesspool. The MPs fished him out when they got there; but just thinking about what it must have been like for poor Pipey makes me shudder; trapped in that deep cesspool with no means of climbing out, and trying to stay alive by keeping his head above its foul and abominable contents before the MP's could rescue him.

He was returned to Ho Tung House where he was no doubt hosed down and given fresh clothes to wear before spending the night in a cell in the guardhouse. He was immediately put on a charge and went on trial next day where he was reduced to the ranks (meaning his rate of pay would be that of a private soldier) for a month.

Pipey appeared at the chanter practice the following day as if nothing had happened. Of course none of us would ever dream of mentioning anything to him about his escapade. A private soldier does not speak to a warrant officer unless he questions him about something, and even then it would only be to answer the question that the officer had asked.

HO TUNG HOUSE

The pipe band made steady progress in both 'On Parade' and 'Off Parade' performances and we played for the regiment on many occasions on the parade ground. The soldiers loved to march to the sound of pipes, it was somehow inspiring to them, and they were magnificent in their soldiering as we watched them march past us. Speaking for myself, I felt extremely proud of them, and in all of these events I always felt the "Esprit de Corps" rise in my breast.

There was one occasion when the pipe band went down to the docks in Kowloon to welcome one of the troopships to Hong Kong. We were dressed in whites for this occasion, white spats and white tunics, and we spent most of the day around the docks waiting for the ship and when it arrived,, we played at intervals for the soldiers while they disembarked.

We were transported to the Kowloon docks by truck; these were the normal troop carrying trucks with benches to sit on. When our engagement was over, our trucks arrived to take us back to Ho Tung House, but this time instead of the normal troop carrying trucks, they sent us coal carrying trucks; what an affront!. Pipey and the other NCO's would go in front with the driver, but the rest of us would be in the back, standing up and holding on to the metal ribs supporting the canvas top. Pipey had noticed the dirty condition of these trucks and he warned not to get our whites soiled as we had another engagement coming up.

The road from the docks to our camp was a twisting and winding, and the travel time was just under an hour. It was only with the greatest of uneasiness and dexterity that we managed to hang on and not get our whites soiled. The only one who managed to solve the problem and relax was the big drummer. He still had the harness on with the large hook that he would hang the big drum onto, so he simply hooked himself on to a top rail and swung back to camp.

Jim in "Whites" and "Royal Stewart" tartan.

The officers in the army are usually seen only on the parade ground or during inspections. They have their own quarters that are quite apart from all the others; they eat and socialize in their own officer's mess where they are waited on by their own mess waiters. They would regularly have a "do" in their mess and amuse each other with some hilarity and antics. At these do's they would ask the pipe major to come and play for them and to have one of the pipers (which would always be John Reid) entertain them with some Highland dancing.

It was a complete surprise when Pipey asked me to accompany him on the pipes at one of these do's, and I felt quite honoured to have been chosen. Pipey went on to tell me what this program at the Mess would be. After the officers meal had been concluded, the tables cleared and the officers glasses filled with the beverage of their choice, we will march into the Mess playing the pipes, and he mentioned a couple of tunes. We will march around the very long table that the officers are sitting at a couple of times, and then stop at the open area at the middle of the table and finish our piece.

Corporal Reid will then lay down his pipes and we will play for him while he danced the "Ghillie Callum". After Corporal Reid has finished, I will lay my pipes down and you will play, while Corporal Reid and I dance a two man Strathspey and Reel. When we have finished the dance, the three of us will start playing again and march round the table twice more. Then you and Corporal Reid will leave the mess by the way we came in and I will stay behind.

Pipey then named the tunes that we would be playing and said that I have a week to practice before Officers Mess. When he had finished describing the order of events he asked:."Any questions?" to which I replied "No Sir." He ended the conversation by saying "All right Ritchie you can fall out." This was typical of the discourse that took place between a private and a senior officer in the British Army.

After listening to Pipey telling me about my participation in this event at the Mess, I started to get a little nervous about the whole thing; I had never played a solo piece before, which I would be doing when Pipey and John were dancing. Would the officers fix me with their usual disdainful looks as I was playing, ? but like it or lump it I had been given an order and there was no way out.

The three of us practiced our routine several times and had everything down pat. The days rolled on, and there we were at the appointed day and hour, standing behind the closed doors of the Officers Mess, dressed in our finest highland dress. I was wearing black brogues, but Pipey and John were wearing their dancing shoes as we waited for the signal to enter. As we stood there, we could hear the din of voices, laughter and the clinking of glasses coming through the closed doors.

There was a lull in the racket inside and we could hear someone announcing our entry. The double doors swung open and in we marched playing "Scotland the Brave". The room was thick with cigar smoke and I could smell the brandy, the officers were all standing and clapping or throwing clenched fists in the air.

It was not at all what I was expecting; these men were real and alive, and not the wooden faced robots I thought I would see. As we circled the tables, the officers were slapping each other on the back, clinking glasses and shouting their heads off. When we stopped playing, the officers sat down at the table as John prepared to dance.

What a rare treat it was to watch John dance while Pipey and I played for him; he was feather light on his feet and executed each step with such precision and grace. He held his head high with a radiant smile lighting up his face; John was indeed the most beautiful of dancers. During this dance, most of the officers at the back of the table had stood up to watch John's footwork, and when he finished, he received a thunderous applause. They had watched John dance before and appreciated the magical talent he possessed.

Pipey then laid down his pipes and went out on the floor facing John. There was thunderous applause again, for Pipey was well known to them. I got my pipes up and played the intro to the Strathspey and then the dance started with them gliding past one another back to back, turning and gliding along to the beat of the music.

I could see that the officers were really enjoying watching this ancient ritual of Highland dancing. As I watched, I could see two of the younger officers taking their shoes off and jumping on the table, facing each other and joining in on the dance. Immediately two other officers jumped up at the other end of this long table and also joined in.

I was impressed at how well these young men were dancing, and I found out later that Pipey had been giving them private lessons.

The Strathspey finished and at the last bar, Pipey gave a loud clap of his hands and we went immediately into the Reel. The reel is a fast dance that requires a lot of space, so the young officers on the table came down and watched as Pipey and John performed the fast and intricate steps which ended with a flourish. Again there was thunderous applause; Pipey and John bowed and came back, picked up their pipes and we stood in a line once again.

At that moment one of the waiters came forward bearing a silver tray with three crystal goblets, each containing a full measure of Scotch. We accepted the goblets and the Lieut. Colonel of the Regiment stood up and proposed a toast to the Queen, to which everyone leapt to their feet, raised their glasses high and shouted "The Queen."

It was over; we got the pipes up and marched around the table twice as arranged, then John and I left the room and Pipey stayed behind to carry on with some serious drinking. Any fears that I had about performing tonight were put to rest; I had enjoyed the evening very much and now had a newfound admiration for the officers of my regiment.

At the beginning of November 1952, we were told that HMS Devonshire, our troopship, had arrived in port, and that after a clean up and spruce up, our regiment would be embarking on that ship, the same one I had come out on, for our trip back to the U.K.

The Pipers in whites, ready for Parade.

This was wonderful news for all of us, especially the National Servicemen like me. Unlike the regular soldier who had volunteered to serve in the army and was paid a reasonable wage for doing so, we on the other hand had been unwillingly recruited into the army; given a two year sentence called National Service, and were paid less than minimum wages for the honour of "serving with the colours". From the very start, most of us had been unwilling participants in this army life and were counting the days when our two-year sentence would be over and we'll once again be free. For me it was still four months before that glorious day would come.

ELEVEN

Troopship Devonshire and Home

Now that the word was out about our regiment shipping back to "Blighty", life at camp was geared towards making preparations for this big move. Stores had to be checked and packed if necessary; all of the soldiers were responsible for making sure that their uniforms were clean and in good order. We had a laundry in the camp run by a local Chinese family, so we could get good laundry service whenever we required it. During our stay in Hong Kong we wore lightweight "Jungle Greens", shorts or longs and jungle shirts, and would continue wearing them on the ship until ordered to change into our regular khaki uniforms, which would happen as the weather got colder.

I handed in two of my shirts for laundering and pressing ten days before our move out date, and it slipped my mind to pick them up until two days before we were leaving. When I handed in my chit at the laundry, the Chinese attendant could only find one of my shirts. The place looked like it had been cleaned out and someone had walked off with one of my shirts. It was too late in the day to file a complaint, so I would just have to get by with two shirts that I still had. I did not know it at the time, but there would be a price to be paid later on for this "loss of equipment".

Pipey told us that we would be carrying our pipes on board, the drums would be in "stores" and we would be playing for the regiment on several occasions during the voyage. The day before our scheduled departure, a complete inspection of the camp was made by the officers and senior NCO's to make sure that the billets and grounds of Ho Tung House were left spic and span for whichever regiment would be moving in to this camp after we left.

The next morning a fleet of trucks arrived and we were quickly transported to the docks at Kowloon, where we were lined up and ordered to stand at ease until our turn came to board the ship. Every man had to carry his own personal belongings on board; all our kit was contained in our Big Pack and our Kit-bag. We also had our rifles,(which would be handed in as we boarded) and the pipers had to carry their cased instruments.

As the ship was the same one that I had sailed on my outward trip, I was fairly familiar with the previous areas where we had eaten and slept, but totally unfamiliar with many parts that were out of bounds to privates like myself. The officers and senior NCO's had separate quarters that were no doubt much superior to ours, but never having seen their quarters I will never know. All I knew was that class distinction was rife in the British army.

After the interminable waiting around that one has to endure in the army, we finally boarded the ship and were led to the deck space that had been allotted to us. This was a step up from my outward trip deck allocation where my squadies and I had been relegated to the fourth and lowest deck at the aft end of the ship. Here we were on the third deck about mid-ships where the layout of the tables and storage areas was exactly the same as down below. We would be sleeping in hammocks again, which is a pretty good way to sleep once you get used to it.

When all our kit had been stored to satisfaction, we were allowed up on deck to say goodbye to Hong Kong and watch as the ship slowly pulled away from the Kowloon dock. The military band of the K.O.S.B.'s were playing a wonderful selection of tunes on deck that were striking a chord in all of us. Many were thinking about the boys who lost their lives and would not be going home with us. Myself, and I am sure all my former squadies were thinking about Ian Coulter whose bones were now lying in a military cemetery in Korea.

The tunes that the band was playing were Scottish, like "Will Ye No Come Back Again", "Annie Lawrie" and "Over the Sea to Skye" and mixed in among them were favourite sing-along tunes like "Pack up Your Troubles" and "We'll Meet Again" where everyone joined in on the singing and the mood became almost festive. The band was great to listen to and they would be playing for us on many occasions during the coming weeks. This was the beginning of our voyage; all of us were happy and in good spirits as we headed out into the South China Sea to begin the six weeks' journey home.

Life on board the troopship quickly followed the same pattern that existed on the way out. A duty squad (four men) would be selected the night before for the next day's duties and they would be responsible for fetching the food to our table from the galley. That would include bringing hot water to the table for us to wash our plates and cutlery.

When the meal was finished and the washing up done, all of us except the duty squad would leave the table to let them clean, dry and return the containers that they had brought the food in, then scrub the table top and the floor under the table. A certain length of time was allowed to accomplish all of this, and when finished, all the others seated at this sixteen man table would come back and line up for inspection.

This inspection would usually be carried out by a junior officer who always finished his inspection by asking the question: "Any complaints?" He never got an answer other than "No Sir," for the food aboard ship was always good.

Pipey kept us busy every morning with band and chanter practice, and we played as a band on several occasions when

TROOPSHIP DEVONSHIRE AND HOME

entering or leaving some of the ports we visited. I cannot recall ever being allowed to leave the ship on that trip back home, especially the Arab ports around the Suez Canal, for Colonel Nasser was still stirring up his people and creating a lot of anti-British feelings around the Canal Zone. Within months, the Suez Canal would be blockaded by Nasser with the sinking of several ships, which almost precipitated a war between Egypt and France/Britain. Thankfully, another war was averted because of the swift action from the United Nations.

Once again, this sea voyage was most enjoyable for the troops on board, with lots of sunbathing in the afternoons and sleeping on deck at nights. We had been given the date when our ship would arrive in Southampton and at that time, the Colonel-in-Chief of our regiment, Princess Alice, the Duchess of Gloucester (I had no idea who this royal lady was) would be on hand at the dock to welcome the regiment back home.

During this voyage, all of us had been busily engaged in letter writing to our folks back home, and these stamped and addressed letters would be dropped off at ports of call as we came to them. Our letters would go on ahead of us, letting our families know when we would be home.

To prepare for the inspection by the Royal Princess, our uniforms and equipment had to be in tip top condition, so a lot of time was spent by everyone on pressing our number one uniforms, polishing brasses and shining boots to a Japanese black-lacquer finish.

※

It was smooth sailing for us on the HMS Devonshire until we passed through the Straits of Gibraltar and into the infamous Bay of Biscay which was known universally for the storms that frequented that body of water. It was now late December and we soon found out that the storm season was in full swing; our fairly small ship had no stabilizers (this was 1952) and we were being tossed about like a cork in a stormy ocean. All of us were confined to our decks and told to make sure that everything movable was securely battened down, and we were ordered to stay there until further orders were issued.

The ship was battling the storm by heaving and corkscrewing, creaking and groaning as we sat at our tables down below hanging on for dear life. This had been going on for several hours now and all of us were getting a little anxious about what was happening above, especially when the lights flickered a couple of times.

What we did not know was that the ship had been radioed by the officials at the dock in Liverpool, telling our Captain that the storm was so bad that it would be impossible to dock there at this time. The Captain was advised to turn his ship around, seek shelter on the lee side of the Isle of Man and stay there until the storm abated. To do this, our Captain would have to turn his ship broadside to these gigantic waves that were pounding us - a tricky and dangerous move.

All of us below knew nothing of this as we sat at our table holding on to it like it was a bucking horse. When the Captain did make his turn, we thought that the ship was going to capsize. It heeled over at a very steep angle and seemed to hang there, and at that moment, a flood of water came pouring down our narrow stairway, our only means of escape - remember now we were three decks down.

Someone shouted "The ship is going down" and we all rose as one and tried to get to the stairway, which was impossible for us, given the steeply sloping deck and the water pouring down on it. It was indeed a frightful moment for all of us before the ship slowly righted itself and we all gave a gasp and let out a cheer.

Two days later we finally sailed up the Mersey Channel and docked at the Liverpool dock. There would be no inspection by Princess Alexandria today, and I found out later that two days before when the ship was within sight of land, the Princess was at the docks, as was the 4th Battalion K.O.S.B. and their pipe band, together with a host of other dignitaries to welcome us back home. When they were told that the ship would be delayed for perhaps two days, the Princess had performed her duties by inspecting the troops of the 4th Battalion K.O.S.B. and their pipe band had played for her. After these ceremonies were over, they all went home.

I also found out later that the Princess had actually come aboard HMS Devonshire when it finally docked, and at a small ceremony aboard welcomed Lt.Col. Tadman and his fellow officers back home. We were told that there would be no inspection by the Princess and we would disembark in due course and that a special troop train would be leaving at 11p.m. to take us all back to Scotland.

It was Christmas Day 1952 and it was a cold one as we looked out from the deck of our ship to a bleak and dreary Liverpool Dock. All of the troops on board had been ready to disembark for hours, all wearing greatcoat and carrying our big pack, our small pack and a fully stuffed kit bag, (our band equipment and uniforms had been left in "Stores") as we finally made our way down the gangplank on to dry land again.

Trucks were lined up for the ride to the railway station where the troop train was waiting to take us back to Scotland. With our bulky baggage, we all crammed into that train wherever we could find an empty seat, and at dusk, we slowly steamed out of the station to begin our all night ride up north over the Borders and into Scotland.

Most of the lads in the small compartment that I was in were smokers, so they lit up right away and soon had the compartment filled with smoke. While I was one of the few non- smokers in our platoon, I had sort of got used to the smoking of others', so it didn't bother me too much. I could see that it seemed to settle all the smokers down quite a bit.

We passed some of the time playing cards but soon lost interest in the game, and before long, all of us dozed off into an uncomfortable and fitful sleep, lulled by the clackity - clack of the carriage wheels.

After what seemed like many hours, I was awakened by someone calling "We are passing over the Border!" Everyone was immediately awake and crowded to the windows. It was dark outside, but we could sense that we were now in Scotland.

A short time later we stopped at Moffat, one of the small border towns on the line, where a crowd of people were assembled holding up a large 'Welcome Home" banner. It had the names of a number of young soldiers from the village written on it, all of whom had been away from home fighting in a foreign land for the best part of two years. A cheer went up as the young men stepped off the train and into the arms of their Mother or sweetheart.

I witnessed the same homecoming reception at several of the stations that we stopped at, and where large numbers of the troops got off; this was Border Country and these were the men from the Kings Own Scottish Borderers coming home to their adoring and beloved families.

From our last stop, it seemed a short time until our now much emptier train steamed into Glasgow Central Station. It was early morning and the sun was shining, but there were no crowds of people waiting to greet those of us who were the last to come off the train. We smiled at one another, shook hands and said we would see each other in three weeks time. (we had three weeks leave coming) We then shouldered our kit bags and went off on our separate ways. I was the only one in the whole regiment who came from the town of Barrhead, so from now on I would be traveling alone. That was good, for it would give me time to think about my own life and situation now that my horizons had been greatly broadened by events of the past many months.

The distance from the railway station to the bus terminal where I would get a bus to Barrhead was a bit of a walk, but it was a lovely morning; I was feeling good and excited to get back home again. I stepped it out, happy to be breathing the fresh air again, after being cooped up in that smoke filled compartment on the train for many hours.

Glasgow had not changed very much during the time I was gone. The stone buildings that lined the streets, some of which were beautiful architectural works of art, were still as black as I remembered them, blackened by the coal burning smoke of the industrial and post industrial revolution years when coal was king and every household, factory and steam train contributed to the soot that was in the air.

Clyde Street, where I would catch the bus, was, as the name implies, adjacent to the River Clyde which was still as polluted as ever; no one would ever dream of swimming in that river. The bus ride to Barrhead took about fifty minutes and it was a nostalgic one for me as the bus passed through the city and then out into the country before approaching Barrhead.

It was Boxing Day in 1952 and two years earlier on Boxing Day of 1950 (a date that I will forever remember) was the day that my Dad had died of a massive coronary while standing at the bus stop, the same bus stop at which I was about to step off in a few moments.

The moment came, and as I was about to get off the bus with my kit-bag over my shoulder, I heard a woman say to her friend: "Some mother will be happy to see her son come home."

The need to wait at this bus-stop for a short while was compelling, so I propped my kit-bag against the wall where my Dad had been propped up after he collapsed, and where I had arrived five minutes later to find him. I kept my emotions in check as I stood there; it was like visiting my Dad's grave, and this moment, in a sense, was part of my homecoming.

I considered walking the mile from that bus stop to our house, and if it wasn't for the weight of my kit bag I would have done that.

The street where I lived was deserted and our house looked the same; the garden was not as neat and tidy as it had been when I left and my Grandfather looked after it. He was gone now and the only people left to greet me were my Mother and my little Sister Grace. I thought that perhaps they both might be at our family shop working, and there would be no one home.

The door was unlocked so I opened it and called out "I'm home!" My Mother immediately came through from the kitchen, she had her apron on and she called out "Oh Jim, you're home, safe and sound!"

We hugged for a long moment; there were no words spoken and no tears, but I felt a great sense of contentment flood over me at being home with my Mother in our family home. I was home, but unfortunately still in the army, and in three weeks time I would be back in a different barracks being ordered around again, and subjected to the daily inspections that was part of the life of a private soldier.

I made the most of my three weeks' freedom by meeting with some of my friends who were now free from their National Service commitment, having just completed their time.

I also dated Jean Campbell who had been writing to me while I had been abroad. She was a lovely petite young woman, very clever, who introduced me to live theatre in the town of Paisley where she lived. She was very keen on live theatre, and I must admit that I did enjoy going to these performances when accompanied by Jean.

Half way through my leave I received a letter from the military authorities ordering me to report to Redford Barracks, a former Cavalry Barracks, located near the village of Penicuik, ten miles south of Edinburgh. The letter contained a bus and rail pass dated for the last day of my leave - they had me on the hook again.

TWELVE

Redford Barracks and Freedom

Upon reporting to Redford Barracks, I was informed that my regiment, the 1st. Btn. K.O.S.B. had been deployed to Northern Ireland to help quell the sectarian violence that was rocking this part of the U.K. and to combat the anti-British terrorist activity that the I.R.A. was conducting.

The I.R.A. was an organization whose aim was to take over the Northern Irish counties by using terrorist activities. They claimed that this part of Ireland was a part of Ireland and not of the U.K., despite the fact that most of the people of Northern Ireland were of Scottish Protestant descent and had lived there for hundreds of years.

I was told that I would not be rejoining the regiment, and my affiliation with that regiment had ended. The news of this came as a bit of a shock; I would perhaps never again see the close friends that I had made in my regiment, but luckily I did have some addresses to fall back on where I could contact some of them. The staff sergeant who was telling me this looked at some papers and went on to say that the term of my National Service would expire in sixty days, and along with some other soldiers who were in the same position as I, we would be affiliated with a company of troops that were presently billeted in Redford Barracks.

With that, I was dismissed and told to report to the orderly sergeant who would fill me in on all the details.

This was going to be a long sixty days in this place if I was going to be treated as I was during my initial sixteen weeks' basic training in Fort George. But on that front, I soon found out that this was not going to be the case; life in Redford Barracks was much more routine and boring. I was soon pleasantly surprised to find that some of my former squadies along with a handful of other young soldiers had also been sent here to this holding tank, for the same reason as me.

I had also found out that six of my former squadies had signed on for regular service of two or more years with the 'Colours'. They had been offered promotion plus an increase in pay that was at least four times greater than a National Serviceman's pay; perhaps they were enjoying this life in the Army, but I suspect they fell for the "carrot" of more money.

One of our squad had obviously taken a shine to the Army and had risen to the rank of Staff Sergeant, but I was told that he was now having a drinking problem. I remembered him as a young man on our squad who, like the rest of us had never been exposed to hard liquor, and here he was after two years in the Army on the verge of becoming an alcoholic. This was not altogether surprising to me, for on many occasions I had seen the drinking binges that soldiers practiced.

Two-day passes were issued to us at the week-end, and we could go home or visit the Army and Navy Club in Edinburgh where good food and entertainment were always available, and for which we had to pay, but the prices were very reasonable. There would be a dance in the Village of Penicuik most Saturday nights and to pass the time several of my squadies and I would go there, but for some reason or other, I was not as thrilled and excited about music and dance that I once had been.

I did go home on several week-ends and would see Jean Campbell every time, and this lovely young lady would cheer me up and take my mind off the boring Army life that I was enduring. This life in the Army was dragging on interminably for me, and I was marking the days towards that great day when I would finally be discharged, and once again walk a free man. I felt like my life was on hold and I could neither go forward or backward, like a prisoner in his cell scratching off the days until his freedom came.

It became apparent to all of the National Servicemen in our squad that there would be no early discharges from this Army; we were going to be kept here until the very last day. Our squad was given given menial work to do, such as picking up garbage around the precinct of the barracks or washing and cleaning up in the cookhouse and dining hall. A company of regular soldiers were still housed in the Barracks who were responsible for maintaining it until the next batch of soldiers moved in. As a squad, we just hung around waiting to be called to perform some duty or other and this included guard house duty at the front gate.

The great day for me arrived on the 13th of March 1953 when I was notified to report to the quartermaster sergeant in the barracks. I was told to be dressed in civilian clothes and turn in all the clothing and equipment that had been in my care, and which I had originally signed for at the beginning my two years' term in Her Majesty's Forces.

Some of the clothing that I had worn in Korea had long since been turned in and signed for; socks, underwear and other miscellaneous clothing had been replaced from time to time. The Army is very fussy about keeping track of everything, and every time some item needed replacing because it was worn out or damaged in some way, you first had to hand in the old item before they would give you a replacement.

I was unaware of the meticulous manner in which the Army kept track of every single item that I had signed for during my two years. I had been very careful with my clothing and equipment and I did not expect anything to be missing, so dressed in my civvies and carrying all my Army clothes and equipment I presented myself to the quartermaster sergeant in his stores building.

He was expecting me and had my file in front of him, ready to check me through. He told me I could keep my boots (two pairs) and socks, but everything else had to be handed in. With the help of two assistants, he then proceeded to unpack all my gear and laid it on a long counter.

When everything was unpacked and laid out, the assistants would examine each piece; if it was damaged or soiled in any way, I would be charged the appropriate cost of cleaning, repairing or replacing it.

The assistants would call out "One greatcoat, good." and the QMS would tick it off his list, and so on, until all of my equipment had been accounted for. Then the sergeant turned around his list for me to see and said "These are the items that you handed in, and these are the items that are unaccounted for, and for those you will be charged."

I looked at the list and there were six items on it: 1 Gully knife, 1 Lanyard, 1 Pyjama top, 1 Jungle green shirt, 1 Cap badge, 1 Housewife. I thought right away at how ungrateful and mean spirited this was, after all I have endured and been subjected to over the past two years in this Army, you are now going to make me pay for these worthless items?

The gully knife and lanyard I barely remember seeing when I first arrived at Fort George to start my sixteen weeks training. They were useless pieces of equipment and I certainly had never had a need to use them. The jungle green shirt was the one that someone had absconded with when I was late picking it up from the laundry at Ho Tung House. The pyjama top is something I never wear, this was an excess piece of clothing in my view and I had used it on the troopship to polish my brasses and to get that spit and polish shine on my boots. I did not have a cloth, nor could I find one anywhere, and as I have mentioned, we had been ordered to get our uniform and boots in tip top shape for our coming inspection by the Royal Princess or face the consequences. The housewife was a small pouch that contained needles and thread, buttons, wool for darning and some safety pins; over the two years I had used up just about everything in it and had discarded the pouch.

The cap badge of the K.O.S.B. I had in my pocket. I was going to keep it as a souvenir; I had spent many hours shining it to perfection and I had sort of grown attached to it and thought that I had earned the right to keep it, but that, it seemed, was against Army regulations. So feeling a little angry at all this nit-picking, I reached into my pocket, withdrew the badge and laid it on the counter and said "Here, you can keep my badge, and tell me what is the rest of this missing stuff going to cost me?" The QMS looked at me and said: "When you were called up, you were loaned twenty pounds sterling of public funds with your kit, and with the exception of your boots and socks, you are required to hand all of your kit back in good order. You will now pay for the items that you have lost; let me see your pay book"

I handed it over and he took down some particulars from it and after a bit of calculating he said to me "This amount will be deducted from your pay book and the balance will be given to you before you depart the Barracks. You will now proceed to the orderly room and speak to Major ? (a name I did not know) who will issue your discharge. That is all."

I looked at the figure that had been deducted from my pay-book and it amounted to well over a week's pay. What a heartless rip off I thought, considering that the rate of pay for a National Service soldier in the 1950's was 28 shillings ($3.36) a week. Of that, I sent 7 shillings home to my Mother, and there was a 2 shillings tax deducted, which left me a weekly pay of 20 shillings to spend on razor blades, shaving soap, Brasso, boot polish and cloths, haircuts and other bits. So you can see that visits to the NAAFI. (Navy, Army and Air Force Institution) for a decent meal were few and far between for me.

In the orderly room I stood at attention before the major who said in a bored voice. "At ease." He then went on to say in an accented Anglified voice: "I have your discharge papers here, but before I give them to you I want to ask if you have enjoyed your two years in the Army, and if you have learned anything in the process."

I was silent, and he barked at me "Speak up!" so I said. "I have learned a lot Sir." He grunted, disregarded my answer, and then went on to say "Your commanding officer has given you a very good testimonial" He was reading from the back of my Certificate of Discharge.

"It says here that your military conduct was very good, and that you have proved yourself to be a good young laddie; you are hard working and reliable, you are sober, trustworthy, industrious and have plenty of initiative. What do you think of that Private Ritchie?"

I said "I think that is good Sir."

The major then got up from his desk and walked around to where I was standing. He held my Discharge Certificate in his hand, lifted it up for me to see, and as he tapped a finger on it he said "If you look at the front here, you will see that you are not totally discharged from service with Her Majesties Forces yet. You still have three and a half years' serving in the Reserves, and you will be required to attend the Army Drill Hall in Barrhead one evening a week. You will also be required to participate in a two week camp every year, as well as the occasional weekend camps, where you will participate and train in field exercises and manoeuvres; do you understand what I am saying?"

I understood full well what he was saying, but started to

NATIONAL SERVICE: "TWO YEARS OF MY LIFE"

say something like "I was unaware..." He immediately cut me off and said in a loud voice "That is irrelevant, it is all here in black and white, and furthermore if you look at the back of your Discharge Certificate, you will see down at the bottom also in black and white, that you are not officially being discharged today, which is the 13th March 1953. You are instead going on what is called Terminal Leave ,which will last until April 5th and which also means that in an emergency, we can pull you back into the Army again, for possibly an indeterminate period of time."

He again asked the same question "Do you understand what I am saying?" Once again I knew full well what he was saying, but I did not wish to continue a one sided conversation with this pompous ass of an officer who was getting his kicks out of demeaning and lording over me, so I simply said "Yes Sir."

He looked at me and said in a laconic voice "Alright Private Ritchie that is all." I immediately snapped to attention, saluted and bawled out "Sir!" did an about turn and quickly left this place before he could think up any more depressing words to throw at me.

A short ways along the hallway was the paymasters office where I showed my pay-book and collected the money that was coming to me which was not very much, but it would have to last me for the time being. From there it was a short trip to the gatehouse and freedom. I was wearing civilian clothes and holding a small suitcase in my hand that contained two pairs of boots, two pairs of socks and some other small personal items. I showed the gate guard my discharge; he smiled and waved me through.

For a moment I felt like I had just been released from prison; the moment passed and I gave a huge smile of contentment, my body felt recharged and I was ready to take on whatever came my way.

Afterword

In conclusion, I would now like to offer a few thoughts after the many years that have passed since the events which I have written about.

Yes, I was certainly glad to be free from the Army after my two years were up; two years of my life and independence had been taken against my will. I had been bullied, insulted and humiliated as never before by a string of NCO's who loved to shove me around, and there was no way for me to avoid this. Add to this the lording over and apparent disdain with which commissioned officers treated the lower ranks.

But even considering all that, I would be hard pressed to think of any other two years of my life where so many things added up to make it perhaps the most exciting and memorable part of my life. What I experienced and had to put up with, made me look at things differently and perhaps shaped me somewhat as a better human being. I was able to tolerate things that seemed intolerable, and at times even see some humour there.

If fate had shown me that I was eligible to avoid National Service, I am sure that I would have jumped at the chance, but I am also sure that my life would have taken a much different path, one that could not possibly have measured up to the present one that I enjoy.

Jim Ritchie
January 15th 2014

Printed in Great Britain
by Amazon